Simon & Schuster's

GUIDE TO
Bulbs

by
Rossella Rossi

Edited by Stanley Schuler

A FIRESIDE BOOK
PUBLISHED BY SIMON & SCHUSTER INC.
New York London Toronto Sydney Tokyo

To Margherita

The author wishes to thank Angelo Naj Oleari for his valuable advice

Simon and Schuster/Fireside
Simon & Schuster Building
Rockefeller Center
1230 Avenue of the Americas
New York, New York 10020

English translation by John Gilbert

Simultaneously published in Italy
by Arnoldo Mondadori Editore S.p.A., Milan
under the title *Tutto Bulbi*

Symbols by Maria Chiara Molinaroli
Drawings by Vittorio Salarolo

Printed and bound in Italy by Officine Grafiche A. Mondadori Editore, Verona

10 9 8 7 6 5 4 3 2 1
10 9 8 7 6 5 4 3 2 1   Pbk.

Library of Congress Cataloging in Publication Data

Rossi, Rossella.
    Simon & Schuster's guide to bulbs.

    Translation of: Tutto bulbi.
    "A Fireside book."
    Bibliography: p.
    Includes index.
    1. Bulbs.   2. Bulbs – Pictorial works.   I. Schuler,
Stanley.   II. Title.   III. Title: Simon and Schuster's
guide to bulbs.
SB425.R78513   1989   635.9'44   89–11651
ISBN 0–671–68788–3
ISBN 0–671–68789–1 (pbk.)

CONTENTS

NOTE

Plants are listed alphabetically by their scientific names according to the binomial system devised by the Swedish botanist Linnaeus (1707–78). According to an internationally accepted code all living organisms are identified by a double epithet. The first word, written in italic with an initial capital letter, refers to the genus and the second, beginning with a small letter, to the species. In some cases the entries refer to an entire genus (*Iris, Lilium, Tulipa*, etc.). Furthermore, some of the entries do not refer to wild (or natural) species but to hybrids. These are derived from the crossing of two species within the same genus (or different forms or variants within the same species) and possess characteristics of both parents. Latin terms are likewise used to describe hybrids, but in this case the name of the genus and the following name of the hybrid are separated by the multiplication symbol × (e.g *Canna* × *hybrida, Hymenocallis* × *festalis*). If the × precedes the first Latin term this signifies that it is a bigeneric hybrid (e.g. × *Crinodonna corsii*).

Beneath the Latin name are the synonyms or alternative scientific names, if applicable, followed by the vernacular or common name, if there is one.

This is followed by the name of the plant family, which groups a number of related genera. Most bulbous plants belong to the families Iridaceae, Amaryllidaceae and Liliaceae.

The origin of the plant is then given, namely the country or geographical region in which the plant grows wild.

A brief description of the plant's characteristic features is then provided. Mention is also made here of associated hybrids and varieties. These are almost always varieties that are artificially obtained, with attributes more suited to cultivation. The horticultural variety, also known as "cultivar," is given in roman typeface inside quotation marks (e.g. *Camassia leichtlinii* 'Atrocaerulea'). The wild varieties, on the other hand, and the subspecies are both given in italics, again with a small initial letter, following the specific name (e.g. *Agapanthus praecox orientalis*).

The next category, the flowering period, is given only approximately. Even in one country there may be different regional climatic conditions that have different effects on the life cycles of the plants concerned.

All matters related to growing and maintaining the plant are dealt with in the next three categories on cultivation, propagation and care. The first of these discusses the relative hardiness of the plant, its ability to withstand frost in winter, the ideal climate required, the recommended type of soil and position, and planting instructions, whether indoors, outdoors or under glass. In some cases mention is made of any likely pests or diseases, but suggestions as to how these should be treated are found in the main introductory text.

Propagation techniques are briefly listed but here again detailed information is contained in the main text.

In the category relating to care of the plant, hints are given as to how to guarantee its survival during the winter, i.e. whether it should be left outdoors or whether it should be lifted from the ground and moved elsewhere, either into the greenhouse or indoors. The indication as to when such operations are best carried out should be interpreted with some flexibility, as in the case of flowering periods.

Finally, where only one species of a genus is discussed and illustrated, mention is made of other important species belonging to the same genus.

KEY TO SYMBOLS

FLOWERING SEASON

 spring

 summer

 autumn

 winter

LIGHT

 sun

 partial shade

 shade

USES

 beds and borders

 rock garden

 pot plant

 cut flowers

 aquatic plant

 climber

BULBOUS PLANTS

Bulbs have solved the problem of survival during adverse seasons – whether they be cold winters or hot, dry summers – in different ways. Annuals rely entirely on seed, which can remain viable for varying periods ranging from a few days to many years and, in some extreme instances, decades or even centuries. Other plants known collectively as bulbous plants, however, can rely in addition on special underground storage organs – bulbs, tubers, corms, rhizomes and tuberous roots. Thanks to these the plants acquire various characteristics that make them particularly suitable for cultivation. Most of these subterranean organs remain dormant for much of the year, so that they can be lifted, transplanted or stored for lengthy periods without too much difficulty. Moreover, the fact that they possess a supply of stored food gives the plants other advantages: they show greater adaptability, at least during the initial stages of growth, and are thus easier to cultivate; they are capable of tolerating a range of climatic conditions. They are also able to bear flowers, given appropriate treatment, even during the winter indoors. Because of these qualities, flower growers have cultivated bulbous plants for many centuries, using wild species to obtain an infinite number of varieties and hybrids.

By trying to identify the environmental conditions that in nature originally led to the evolution of bulbous plants, we have learned that they often have very different ecological requirements. Many tulips of Asiatic origin, for example, are adapted to an extreme continental climate, with brief rainfall in spring and hot, dry summers. Certain fritillaries, on the other hand, live on swampy ground. And there are many woodland species, such as snowdrops, scillas and erythoniums, which, thanks to their food reserves, grow very rapidly and complete their annual cycle by early spring, before the leaves of the trees have had time to develop, drawing warmth and, above all, light from the sun.

The organs of the so-called bulbous plants vary considerably in both structure and function.

True bulbs are a sort of plant in embryo, consisting of a very short basal disk of tough tissue, the basal plate, with a shoot protected by modified white and fleshy leaf bases known as scales. The scales contain stored food reserves: starch, sugar, and some proteins. From the basal plate sprout thin, adventitious roots. In many cases the bulbs are protected and covered by dry brown, white or black skins that constitute the tunic. Bulbs, with few exceptions (e.g. *Cardiocrinum*), are perennial and renew annually the food stored in the scales. Bulbs are typically represented by the onion (*Allium cepa*).

(Stem) tubers are swollen underground stems modified in order to perform their storage function. Covered by a tough skin, they are almost wholly constituted, inside, of food substances. On the surface are latent buds (eyes), from which, when conditions are right, shoots of the new plants will sprout. A typical tuber is the potato (*Solanum tuberosum*).

Corms are outwardly similar to tubers but consist of a much larger proportion of stem tissue. Whereas in bulbs it is the adapted leaf bases (scales) that perform the storage function, in corms the leaves are thin and much smaller, and all the food reserves are accumulated in the fleshy stem, from the base of which the roots also develop. In the upper

Basic characterisics of tubers (above), rhizomes (center), and tuberous roots (below).

Overleaf: the vegetative cycle of all bulbous plants follows a precise reproductive process, formed by stages that vary according to whether they are true bulbs (e.g. Begonia x tuberhybrida), *rhizomes (e.g.* Canna x hybrida), *or tuberous roots (e.g.* dahlia x cultorum)

part, protected by modified leaves, one or two buds are visible, and these constitute the new plants. Unlike bulbs, corms exhaust their food reserves with every growth cycle. They are transformed into dry disks, and are replaced by completely new corms of flowering size plus several tiny brand new corms called cormels. Examples of plants with corms are gladioli, crocus, and erythronium.

Rhizomes are adapted, often thickened underground stems that grow horizontally. Their upper part produces leaves and flower stalks and their lower part, roots. Anemones and most iris are plants furnished with rhizomes.

Tuberous or fleshy roots or root tubers are genuine roots transformed into fleshy storage organs and no longer able to perform their original absorbent function, which is carried out by other nutritive roots that are of normal appearance. The buds are as a rule found on the collar, at the base of the aerial stem. Plants with tuberous roots include dahlias and ranunculus.

THE GROWTH CYCLE

Although times and methods may vary, the life cycles of plants, including the bulbous species, have gradually evolved and been modifed in order to carry out in the most efficient possible manner a single task: regeneration or, in other words, continuation of the species. There are several steps in this growth process.

As soon as temperature and moisture conditions become favorable, bulbs, corms, tubers, rhizomes, and tuberous roots emerge from their dormant condition and resume their plant growth. As a rule, the first part to develop is the root system, which has to perform the double function of anchoring the plant in the soil and absorbing water and mineral salts from the ground. Only when the roots are well established do the aerial parts appear, and these have the task of guaranteeing, by means of the flower and the seeds, sexual reproduction, and of ensuring, through the leaves, the synthesis and accumulation of food reserves, including those needed for flowering the following year. For this reason it is important that the roots are not disturbed or damaged in the growing season.

If conditions are unfavorable, the bulbs continue to develop underground, using their energy stocks to create secondary, lateral bulbs or new scales around the tunic. Some lilies and fritillaries can, especially in mild winters, remain dormant for the whole season.

Seed production involves the union, by means of the stigma, which collects the pollen, of the male cell, produced by the anthers, and the female cell, enclosed in the pistil. But plants have another way of ensuring continuation of the species: vegetative or agamic reproduction. The progeny thus produced are always identical to the parent plant, for there is no inherited genetic exchange between different individuals. Among bulbous plants in the wild, vegetative reproduction is mainly carried out by bulbs and corms developing offsets of varying size that can be detached to lead an independent life. This phenomenon is typically evident in narcissi and tulips. Certain species of the genus *Lilium* and *Calo-*

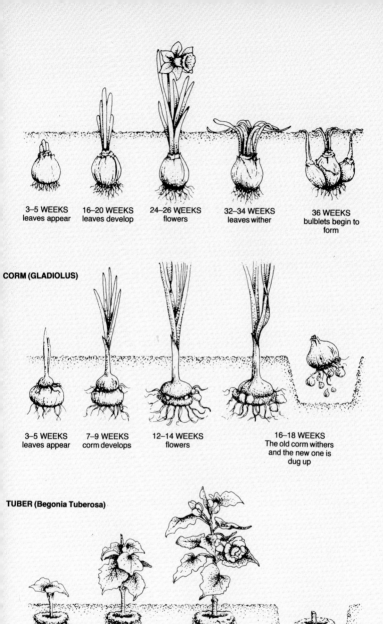

3–5 WEEKS
leaves appear

16–20 WEEKS
leaves develop

24–26 WEEKS
flowers

32–34 WEEKS
leaves wither

36 WEEKS
bulblets begin to
form

CORM (GLADIOLUS)

3–5 WEEKS
leaves appear

7–9 WEEKS
corm develops

12–14 WEEKS
flowers

16–18 WEEKS
The old corm withers
and the new one is
dug up

TUBER (Begonia Tuberosa)

3–5 WEEKS
leaves appear

7–9 WEEKS
leaves develop

12–14 WEEKS
flowers

AFTER FIRST FROST
tuber should be
dug up

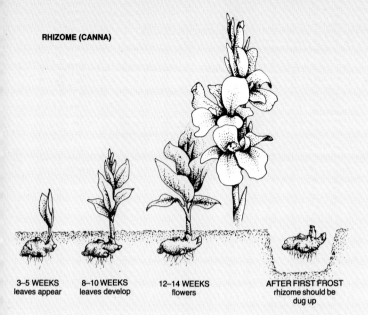

RHIZOME (CANNA)

3–5 WEEKS
leaves appear

8–10 WEEKS
leaves develop

12–14 WEEKS
flowers

AFTER FIRST FROST
rhizome should be
dug up

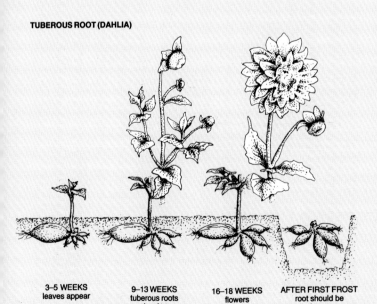

TUBEROUS ROOT (DAHLIA)

3–5 WEEKS
leaves appear

9–13 WEEKS
tuberous roots
develop

16–18 WEEKS
flowers

AFTER FIRST FROST
root should be
dug up

chortus have the additional ability to produce small bulbs in the leaf axils. Soon after the termination of flowering, these bulbils detach themselves from the mother plant, fall to the ground and, should the surrounding conditions be favorable, produce a bulb capable in its turn of flowering.

Some species of tulip (e.g. *Tulipa sylvestris*) throw out stolons or runners, which may be up to 28 in (70 cm) long, from the base of the bulbs, and new bulbs form from their tips.

Rhizomes, too, are efficient colonizers, as in the case of the iris. They grow to invade the surrounding area and a new plant originates from each node.

BULBS IN LEGEND AND HISTORY

Many bulbous plants are inextricably linked to important periods in human history. The manioc, the sweet potato, and the yam, for example, have for centuries been the staple item of diet for a large number of primitive people. The leek and the onion were highly valued by the ancient Egyptians, and the potato has always been of vital importance to the Indians of South America. Saffron, obtained from the pistils of *Crocus sativus*, was an important commercial product for the Minoans, who exported it throughout the then-known world. It was not only a spice but also a powdered dyestuff, an aromatic substance and an effective drug. It was as a rule highly prized, which is not surprising because 8,000 flowers are required to produce about 2 oz (50 g) of powder.

Other species have acquired significance because of their esthetic qualities. The iris – probably *Iris pseudacorus* – was for a long time the symbol of the French monarchy. The lily (*Lilium candidum*), known in ancient Crete and in the age of Solomon's temple, had a ritual importance for the Greeks, being sacred to Hera, goddess of purity. According to tradition, however, Aphrodite maliciously provided it with its pistil, an obvious phallic symbol. For that reason, the lily, which in Christian iconography frequently appears in the hand of the Angel of the Annunciation as the symbol of purity, is often depicted without a pistil.

The plant with the most extraordinary associations is the tulip. Unmentioned by the great classical authors such as Dioscorides, Theophrastus, and Pliny, who evidently did not know it, the tulip was cited by thirteenth- and fourteenth-century Persian poets, and was by 1500 a recurrent ornamental motif. But it was a Flemish diplomat, Ogier Ghislain de Busbecq, ambassador of the Austrian Emperor Ferdinand I at the court of Sultan Suleiman the Magnificent in Constantinople, who was the first European to recognize the plant's existence. This happened in 1554 when, in an Adrianapolis street, he was astonished by the beauty of these lovely flowers, which were in bloom during the depths of winter. He discovered, too, that the Turks were prepared to pay huge sums of money to purchase the rarest and most beautiful varieties. Soon afterwards tulips made their triumphant entry into the imperial gardens of Vienna.

A few years later the Flemish botanist Carolus Clusius moved from Austria to Leiden in Holland. He took with him bulbs of the valued plant;

and subsequently, though in a most unusual manner, the tulip won universal fame. Clusius planted the prized bulbs in his own garden, but for quite some time resisted the inquiries and extravagant financial offers of other people who wanted to acquire the flowers. Indeed, it was only after someone broke into his garden one night and stole both flowers and bulbs that a flourishing trade was inaugurated. Then it was not long before someone else realized that tulips, when propagated vegetatively from bulbs, could produce in later generations individuals with variegated and bizarre colors, apparently having nothing in common with their parents. (Only in the nineteenth century was it discovered that this phenomenon was usually due to a virus.) The result was a frenzied race to acquire bulbs that could, in theory, yield virtually every kind of surprise. During 1634–37 prices went up steadily, and what became known as "tulipomania" eventually gripped the entire Dutch population, high and low alike. At a certain point, however, the market became saturated and prices suddenly collapsed. Symbolizing the end of tulipomania is the image of a certain professor Evrard Forstius, who was in the habit of destroying with his walking-stick any tulips that he happened to encounter in his daily jaunts. Or it may be that tulipomania never really died, because Dutch growers still produce and sell thousands of millions of bulbs every year.

HOW TO USE BULBOUS PLANTS

Even the smallest plot of ground can be used profitably to accommodate bulbous plants. Indeed, there are so many species and varieties now on the market as to satisfy almost any contingency. There are species that flower in the autumn, or even in the winter; species for shady or sunny spots, for wet or dry soils, for the rock garden, for climbing or trailing, and so forth. Virtually any garden, if planned patiently and sensibly, can be transformed to provide flowers all year round; and it is not necessary to be a professional to achieve excellent results. What is most important is to find out as much as you can about the area you intend to set aside for the purpose: previous history, nature of soil, average temperatures, seasonal minimum and maximum temperatures, exposure to sun, prevailing winds, etc. After that it is a question of selecting and buying those plants that best suit your situation. This is perhaps the most difficult part of the process but not an impossible one. Each plant has its particular requirements and you must take this into consideration. The follwoing tables and, more especially, the plant entries that comprise the greater part of this book serve as a useful guide. But the most important factor of all is individual experience. The best advice can only point the way, suggesting methods of procedure, and providing a framework on which to base your own efforts.

Beds and borders. Almost all species described in this book are suitable for creating beds and borders. Naturally you must take account of climatic requirements, size (the smallest species should be planted at the front), colors, etc. Remember, too, that some plants are particularly

Anemone, with white flowers, surrounded by Agapanthus. Both these genera are particularly suitable for flowering borders.

showy and decorative, and so deserve pride of place. Among these are *Cardiocrinum giganteum* (giant lily), *Eremurus robustus* (Foxtail lily), etc.

Plants for naturalizing. A species is suitable for naturalizing when it reproduces and spreads easily of its own accord to form extensive colonies. For this to happen, its ecological needs must be fully satisfied. Success generally depends on using hardy species that flourish in the wild in similar surroundings, and on planting initially a reasonable number of individuals. This practice is particularly suitable in large gardens with areas that can be left to grow wild, or in a woodland setting.

The following genera are especially easy to naturalize:

Allium	*Endymion*	*Muscari*
Anemone	*Erythronium*	*Narcissus*
Arum	*Fritillaria*	*Ornithogalum*
Colchicum	*Galanthus*	*Scilla*
Crocus	*Leucojum*	*Sternbergia*
Cyclamen	*Lilium*	*Tulipa*

Spring-flowering plants. Although one can find different bulbs to flower at almost any time of the year, spring is the season when the majority of the species are in flower. The season starts with snowdrops

Allium flavium. *A summer-flowering variety particularly suitable for flowering borders.*

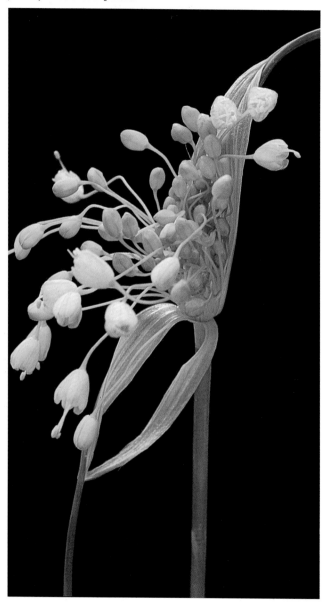

Galanthus), crocuses (*Crocus*) and winter aconites (*Eranthis*), continues with grape hyacinths (*Muscari*) and fritillaries (*Fritillaria*), and concludes with the hyacinths (*Hyacinthus*). The following is a list of more common hardy genera that produce spring flowers:

Allium	*Eranthis*	*Muscari*
Arum	*Eremurus*	*Narcissus*
Asphodelus	*Erythronium*	*Ornithogalum*
Bulbocodium	*Fritillaria*	*Puschkinia*
Camassia	*Galanthus*	*Ranunculus*
Convallaria	*Hyacinthus*	*Scilla*
Crocus	*Iris*	*Trillium*
Cyclamen	*Leucojum*	*Tulipa*

Summer-flowering plants. Most of the bulbous species that flower in summer are not hardy. They often therefore have to be planted out in spring, after there is no further danger of late frost, and dug up and stored over winter. Some can be grown outside only in temperate or warm zones. The following is a list of the best-known summer-flowering genera:

Achimenes	*Dierama*	*Pancratium*
Acidanthera	*Eucomis*	*Paradisea*
Agapanthus	*Galtonia*	*Polianthes*
Allium	*Gladiolus*	*Sinningia*
Alstroemeria	*Gloriosa*	*Sparaxis*
Amaryllis	*Haemanthus*	*Sprekelia*
Anemone	*Hymenocallis*	*Tigridia*
Begonia	*Iris*	*Triteleia*
Calochortus	*Ixia*	*Tritonia*
Canna	*Lapeirousia*	*Vallotta*
Chlidanthus	*Lilium*	*Watsonia*
Crinum	*Lilium*	*Zantedeschia*
Crocosmia	*Lycoris*	*Zephyranthes*
Dahlia	*Moraea*	

Autumn-flowering plants. As well as plants that usually flower in autumn, such as autumn crocuses and colchicums, which will produce flowers until the first frosts, or *Sternbergia*, whose flowers appear in September–October and last one or two weeks, there are those that go on flowering until the frosts arrive. Among these, the best-known and most useful are the dahlias. The following is a list of the commonest genera producing autumn flowers:

Acidanthera	*Cyclamen*	*Vallotta*
Amaryllis	*Dahlia*	*Zephyranthes*
Colchicum	*Nerine*	
Crocus	*Sternbergia*	

Plants for the rock garden. The rock garden can be a delightful feature. Even within a restricted space, with careful planning and imagination, it is possible to grow a large number of species in a variety of different situations. The only limiting factors, of course, are height and hardiness. Dwarf species are usually more suitable to the rock garden. However, if conditions were suitable, and the rock garden sufficiently large, taller genera such as lilies would also be successful. The following genera are particularly suitable:

Allium	Cyclamen	Muscari
Anemone	Eranthis	Ornithogalum
Anthericum	Erythronium	Oxalis
Bellevalia	Fritillaria	Puschkinia
Bulbocodium	Galanthus	Romulea
Camassia	Hyacinthus	Scilla
Chionodoxa	Ipheion	Sternbergia
Colchicum	Iris (dwarf)	Tulipa
Corydalis	Ixiolirion	
Crocus	Merendera	

Cut flowers. Many bulbous plants produce flowers that are ideal for cutting. If the operation is carried out with a pair of secateurs or a sharp knife, preferably in the evening and without damaging the leaves, there is no reason why the plant should be harmed. Dirty (i.e. unsterilized) knives or secateurs (shears) may transmit virus infections from one infected plant to a clean one. This can be especially catastrophic with bulbous plants.

The following genera are especially suitable for cut flowers:

Acidanthera	Eucharis	Ixiolirion
Allium	Freesia	Lilium
Alstroemeria	Gladiolus	Narcissus
Clivia	Hermodactylus	Nerine
Crocosmia	Homeria	Sparaxis
Dahlia	Iris	Tulipa
Eremurus	Ixia	

CULTIVATION

Buying plants. There is no problem today in purchasing bulbs. The most common species are sold in garden centers, by mail order and in large stores; the rarer species can usually be ordered direct from specialist firms that issue annual illustrated catalogs. In all cases, but especially if prices are low and there is no guarantee of quality, it is sensible to observe a few simple rules. Bulbs and corms should be sound and whole, with no signs of damage, bruising or discoloration, firm and plump to the touch and relatively weighty. If they seem too light, this may be a sign of disease or dehydration. Should you be in doubt, particularly when purchasing large quantities, it is worth cutting a sus-

pect bulb in half beforehand to check that it looks all right inside.

Having bought the bulbs, it is always a good idea to get them into the ground or potted up as soon as possible, especially if they have not been adequately packed. Bulbs protected by tunics, like those of hyacinths, daffodils, and tulips, can be kept for some time loose in shallow trays. Those without tunics, or those with fleshy, persistent roots (iris) or tubers (cyclamens) or certain other genera, especially woodland species (e.g. Trillium, Erythronium, Eranthis, etc.), desiccate much more quickly and should not remain exposed too long to the air; but they can be kept for short periods in pots or trays filled with sand or moist peat.

Preparing the ground. The ground must, above all, be well dug over. Large stones or rubble and perennial weeds should be removed and clods of soil carefully broken up. The majority of bulbous plants need a light soil of medium texture or slightly sandy, porous, fertile and well drained. It is worth explaining what these terms mean. "Light" as opposed to "heavy" does not refer to specific weight but to ease of working. "Medium loam" alludes to the texture or grain, i.e., to the size of the mineral particles present in the soil in their state of complete dispersion. Internationally accepted convention distinguishes the skeleton comprising particles with a diameter of more than $^3/_{32}$ in (2 mm), and the fine soil, made up of particles with a diameter of less than $^3/_{32}$ in (2 mm). Fine soil, in its turn, consists of gravel, grit, coarse sand, fine sand, silt and clay particles, in varying proportions. Each category is identified with reference to the dimensions of the particles, which have decreasing diameters $^3/_{16}-^3/_8$ in (5−10 mm) in gravel to almost infinitesimal size in clays.

Sandy soils contain 70–80% sand and clay soils more than 25–30% clay. The ideal composition, agriculturally, of so-called medium-consistency soils is 45–80% sand, 10–15% mud, 5–10% clay, 1–5% limestone and 3–5% organic material.

Porosity is a measurement of the percentage of pores and interstices present in the soil. Medium porosity is around 50%. It is slightly lower in sandy soils (30–40%); slightly more in clay soils (55–60%); and at its maximum in humus soils (70–80%).

Another important characteristic is the capacity of water to drain away and not accumulate and so form pools or cause erosion of sloping surfaces, in which case the soil is said to be heavy, compacted or impermeable. Very few bulb species, except for the water-lilies and callas, tolerate or require soils in which water accumulates freely. In badly structured clay soils, which may be most prone to these disadvantages, it may be necessary, while preparing them, to add correctives in the form of sand, well-rotted manure or leafmold to improve drainage. In certain cases it may even be wise to dig ditches or install drainage tiles to drain the soil.

In hopeless situations, one solution is to replace the existing soil entirely or to build raised beds filled with topsoil you buy.

Feeding. Plants, through their root systems, take from the soil the water and mineral salts they need for growth. There are twelve indispensable elements. Some of these, namely boron, manganese, copper, zinc and molybdenum – the so-called trace elements – are absorbed in infinitesimal quantities and appear exclusively in the composition of certain enzymes. These are seldom in short supply. On the other hand, calcium, magnesium, sulfur, iron, nitrogen, phosphorus and potassium are essential structural elements – the macroelements; and while the first four are rarely in short supply, nitrogen, phosphorus and potassium, if present in insufficient quantity, may constitute factors that limit growth. Feeding is aimed at rectifying the balance of these basic nutrients.

Nitrogen constitutes 1–3% of the dry weight of mature tissue and 5–6% of the dry weight of young tissue. It is part of the composition of proteins, of chlorophyll and of nucleic acids, which have the task of fixing hereditary characteristics, and of other important substances such as alkaloids and glucosides. It is absorbed in large amounts during the entire vegetative cycle, particularly during the phases of root development and the flowering and fruiting.

A regular addition of nitrogen needs to be given to all soils that are regularly cultivated. Excluding for the moment organic fertilizers, which will be mentioned later, nitrogen can be administered in inorganic form as calcium cynamide, urea, ammonium sulfate, etc. The best time to apply these is generally in spring, when growth starts – a period when the plant is greedy for this mineral and its availability in the soil is usually in short supply because the biological processes of decomposition of organic material will shortly be resumed. Nitrogen fertilizers assist plant development and the formation of foliage but, if overdone, may have negative effects.

Phosphorus, too, plays a fundamental role in the life of the plant; it is part of the composition of nucleic acids, the molecules responsible for chlorophyll synthesis and energy exchanges. Moreover, it is a valuable storage substance in seeds, tubers, etc. Phosphorus is regarded as an important developmental factor inasmuch as it accelerates and encourages phenomena associated with flowering, fertilization and ripening of fruits. Bonemeal and superphosphate are excellent and widely used sources of phosphorus.

Potassium constitutes 1% of the dry weight of plant tissue and plays a part in all the mechanisms regulating the semi-permeability of the cell membranes, in the maintenance of basic acid equilibrium, in the formation and accumulation of storage substances, and in resistance to harm caused by cold and other adverse conditions. A balanced potassium fertilizer, using potassium chloride, potassium sulfate or potassium salts, will strengthen the stems, promote plant health and influence the color and scent of flowers.

For convenience inorganic fertilizers are often administered, not individually, but in combinations of two or three elements. As a rule the name of such mixed fertilizers is followed by numbers that indicate the principal constituents. The first number shows the percentage content of nitrogen, the second of phosphoric anhydride, and the third of potassium oxide. Thus a three-part mixture labeled 6—12—6 contains 6% nitrogen, 12% phosphoric anhydride and 6% potassium oxide.

Special foliar plant foods (foliar feeds) are sold in preparations designed to be assimilated directly by the leaves. Apart from nitrogen, phosphorus and potassium, these products will often contain trace elements and prove particularly useful in cases of general weakness, which are likely to follow transplanting or as a consequence of frost, hail, prolonged drought, etc.

Organic fertilizers. Although the application of inorganic fertilizers, if properly carried out, has evident and immediate effects on plant growth and health, successful results over a long period depend on the presence or organic material in the soil. In natural surroundings that are not subjected to human exploitation, the residues of plants and dead animals are continually returned to the soil, where, thanks to the combined action of various organisms and micro-organisms, they are progressively decomposed and biochemically modified, eventually being transformed into a blackish, amorphous substance, resistant to further breaking down, known as humus. This is the substance that exerts beneficial effects on the physical and chemical properties of the soil, particularly its structure, aeration, friability and water-holding capacity. Furthermore, humus produced by degradation of organic material is rich in those elements indispensable to plant growth.

Whereas in nature the soil is spontaneously supplied with organic material, it is obvious that in the case of cultivated soil, especially where the crop is regularly harvested, a supplementary supply of organic material has to be provided. These added materials do not always induce the same effects. Thus materials rich in lignin and cellulose, like straw, have a much more positive effect on soil structure but far less on the nutrition of the plant. On the other hand, grass, leaves and wet material in general decompose rapidly and thus release nutrients that are readily used by plants. Among the most valuable organic additives are manures and garden composts. For pot plants, peat is useful for improving

Opposite: a decorative display of Colchium.
*Phosphate fertilizers favor flowering and the
maturing of fruit.*

the structure and water-holding capacity of the compost, and dried blood is helpful if you want to provide a boost of nitrogen (but remember that too much nitrogen can be a bad thing if applied at the wrong time).

Manure consists of a mixture of animal droppings and waste matter left to rot before use. It will eventually be transformed into a uniformly soft, black, odorless mass, in which the original constituents are hard to identify. Although you can use manures before they have decomposed, they can be especially useful when they have rotted down. As a rule manure is dug in during the autumn so that its decomposition is well advanced by spring, when plant growth resumes. If it is already decomposed, don't be afraid to use it in spring. The beneficial effects of manures last several years.

Garden compost is obtained by forming a compost heap in which the heat generated, and the micro-organisms, organic refuse, and plant material decompose with a certain amount of soil. You can also add manure. Garden compost is very effective, and isn't difficult to make if the heap is big enough and you can ensure that it heats up sufficiently.

Peat is a material of natural origin accumulated over the centuries, in particular acid substrata (peat bogs) characterized by a lack of oxygen and by the presence of excessive moisture. Peat is often used in potting composts because it retains water, but it is equally valuable in the garden, for improving soil structure and moisture retention.

Improving the soil. The degree of acidity in the soil has a very evident conditioning effect on the life and health of plants. The extent to which the several nutritive elements are available and assimilated, like the activities of the micro-organisms responsible for the mineralization of organic material, varies considerably according to the acidity or alkalinity of the soil. In many cases, therefore, it may be necessary to adjust the pH (the measure of alkalinity or acidity). The most effective way to correct acidity is to apply lime in the form of calcium carbonate, quicklime (U.S.A.), hydrated lime and ground limestone (Britain) in varying doses according to the situation. Too much alkalinity can be corrected by adding plenty of organic material such as manure, garden compost, and peat (which is acid). You can also use powdered sulfur. Acidic fertilizers such as sulfate of ammonia will also reduce the alkalinity (but only use these if the fertilizer is actually needed).

You may also need to improve soil structure and texture. The application of manure, garden compost, or peat is usually the most effective and simple remedy, whether the soil is too loose or too compact. Sand can also be added over small areas to improve texture and correct clay soils. Liming generally has a beneficial effect on heavy soils, but don't apply it if the ground is already alkaline.

Planting bulbs outside. There are three basic methods of planting bulbs outdoors. The first is to plant single specimens in a lawn or alongside other bulbs, using a special trowel (bulb-planter) to remove cylinders of earth to any required depth. The holes are filled in after you have placed individual bulbs in the bottom. Alternatively, you could use an ordinary trowel, which is much quicker if the ground is already soft and

workable, and it is easier to make shallow holes. The third method is particularly suitable for planting uniform groups of bulbs, and involves the removal, with a spade, of a rectangle of soil, of a sufficient size and depth to accommodate the number and types of bulbs intended for planting. Sprinkle a little bonemeal over the bottom, add a thin layer of soil and place the bulbs next to one another, suitably distanced, then re-cover them all.

As regards the depth at which the various kinds of bulbs, corms, tubers, rhizomes or tuberous roots should be planted, consult the entries, but with this proviso: the suggestions need not be followed absolutely to the letter. Broadly speaking, planting should be deeper in sandy soils which are likely to undergo dehydration in hot, dry periods, and less deep in compact or heavy soils. However, if bulbs are not planted deep enough, there is almost bound to be trouble later. In nature the bulbs of certain species may be found as deep as 16 in (40 cm).

In any event, make sure that bulbs are planted at a depth equal to two or three times their greatest diameter.

The planting distance is quite flexible. Much depends on the effect desired. For natural groups of crocuses, snowdrops and cyclamen, 2–4 in (5–10 cm) is enough. Larger species such as gladioli, hyacinths, and iris will need more space, e.g. 4–8 in (10–20 cm).

Time of planting must be based on the flowering season. In general, all hardy spring-flowering species should be planted in autumn. This group includes the best-known bulbous plants such as tulips, lilies, narcissi, lilies of the valley, fritillaries, etc.

Other hardy species that flower in autumn should be planted in summer. This is also the most suitable time for transplanting species that have a very short dormancy period, including colchicums, autumn crocuses and daffodils, *Nerine*, *Amaryllis*, etc.

Finally, the tender summer-flowering species need to be planted in spring, when there is no further risk of frost. Among these are *Acidanthera*, *Hymenocallis*, *Dahlia*, *Tigridia*, etc.

Watering. An expert eye is required to tell exactly how much water plants need at the various stages of their development. As a rule, they require maximum amounts at the time of flowering, especially if this occurs at the height of summer, as in the case of lilies and gladioli. Pot-grown species are particularly likely to suffer from water shortage because their compost dries out much more quickly.

In years of less than average rainfall, supplementary watering may be necessary for the hardy spring-flowering species.

Furthermore, it is absolutely essential not to neglect the foliage after the plants flower. The leaves should not be left to die prematurely, as they help to provide the bulbs with nutrients, and improve the chances of a good display next year.

There are some additional basic rules for watering: ideally, the water should not be too hard, nor should it be sprayed too violently, as this may lead to soil erosion and exposure of the plant roots. In summer, try to avoid watering during the hottest part of the day.

Final stages of growth and winter protection. All expert gardeners

There are three principal methods to lay bulbs in the ground: 1. by means of a special trowel (bulb-planter); 2. a garden trowel; 3. a spade. On the right, a particular kind of bulb-planter.

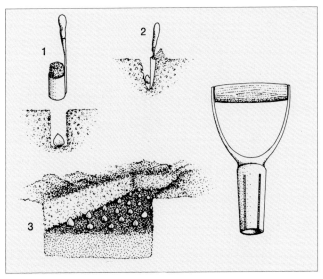

know that it is standard practice to cut off flowers when they begin to fade. The plants do not waste energy producing seeds. However, great care must be taken not to damage the leaves until they wither completely. In fact, this is the only way to give the plant time and opportunity to store essential substances in its underground organs. It uses up a great deal of energy while flowering, and through photosynthesis the foliage replenishes it.

Once the growth cycle is over, thought has to be given to the months ahead. Not all plants are equally well able to tolerate winter cold. The so-called hardy species, which include most crocuses, narcissi, tulips, scillas and many others, will survive without problem at below-zero temperatures. On the other hand, slightly tender plants that are not grown in particularly well-sheltered spots need special protection during the winter. This is provided by covering the ground with dry leaves, straw, wood chips, pulverized bark, or similar materials. The purpose of this mulch is to provide insulation and reduce chances of frost penetrating too deeply, avoid it warming up and encouraging plant growth during unseasonable winter warm periods (this is more likely in some parts of the U.S.A. than in Britain). This mulch should be left in place until just before the plants normally start to make growth in the spring, when there is no further chance of late frost. Among these are *Acidanthera*, *Gloriosa*, *Tigridia* etc.

Keeping bulbs. When the growing season is over, and before the winter cold strikes, bulbs, corms, tubers, rhizomes and tuberous roots of

The table below indicates the depth, and relative position, at which to plant some of the more common summer bulbs: Agapanthus, whose fleshy rhizomes should be placed just below the surface of the soil and in a vertical

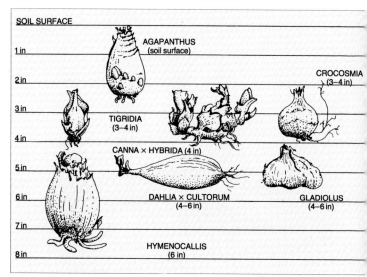

tender species should be lifted from the ground and sheltered until spring. The individual requirements of these species are mentioned in the entries. In all cases, however, let the bulbs and other underground organs dry out for ten days or so in any airy position, then discard damaged or diseased bulbs, clean off the soil, treat with a fungicide and place in shallow, open trays filled with peat or vermiculite. It is important to take care that the bulbs do not touch one another in order to prevent the possibility of rotting. Provide protection against mice, with wire mesh. Dahlias should be stored at a temperature of 41°–45°F (5°–7°C); *Achimenes* at 57°–59°F (13°–14°C); and at 63°–65°F (17°–18°C) for many Iridaceae and Amaryllidaceae, such as *Tigridia*, *Acidanthera*, *Tigridia*, etc., which come from countries where temperature variations during the entire year are very slight and which therefore cannot stand low temperature levels, at 63°–65°F (17°–18°C).

PROPAGATION OF CULTIVATED BULBOUS PLANTS

There are two methods of propagating plants: from seed (gamic multiplication) or vegetatively (agamic multiplication).

Seed propagation. This is sexual reproduction, which occurs as a result of the union of two cells: a male, produced by the male reproductive organ, namely the stamens, and a female, contained in the female reproductive organ, namely the ovary. The process, in brief, is as fol-

position, Dahlia, whose tuberous roots should be covered with circa 4–6 in (10–15 cm) of soil and placed in a horizontal position, Lilium (4–8 in [10–20 cm], vertical) and Galtonia (6 in [15 cm], vertical).

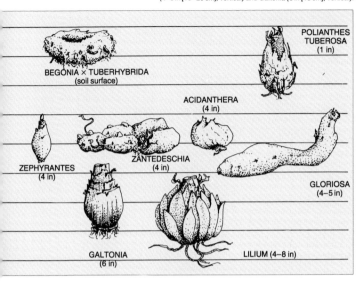

lows: The pollen grains, released by the anthers, find their way, thanks to insects, wind and other agents, to the tip of the female reproductive organ, the stigma, and penetrate inside to carry out fertilization. At this point a series of occurrences leads to the production of the seed, which is an embryo provided with stocks of food substances and covered by a protective tegument. The seeds differ greatly in appearance, form and size. They may be naked or protected by the fruit.

Fertilization ensures that there is a continual mingling of the hereditary factors belonging to different individuals – basically between those of the same species. This establishes an evolutionary pattern that works in favor of certain characteristics and to the detriment of others. In floriculture the continual modifications of characteristics that result from sexual reproduction are only of consequence if they serve to create new varieties. Otherwise it is preferable for the different plant species or varieties to remain, as far as possible, unaltered. For this reason growers tend to resort more frequently to vegetative propagation in order to obtain individuals guaranteed to be exactly identical to their single parent. Another reason for growers not to rely too closely on seeds is that the majority of bulbous plants obtained from seed do not flower for 4–5 years. *Cardiocrinum giganteum*, in fact, takes 7 years. There are, of course, exceptions: dwarf dahlias, for example, sown in February–March, will flower the same year, while freesias need 6–12 months before flowering.

Sowing seed. Seeds have a highly variable capacity for survival and may retain their characteristics unaltered for several days, for months or for years, according to the species producing them and the manner in which they have been kept. In order to germinate, therefore, they need very well defined conditions of temperature, aeration and moisture. As a rule, the seeds of bulbous plants, which require a number of years to flower, are never set directly outdoors but sown in pots or seed trays, at the bottom of which is placed a layer of shards (broken crocks) or other material that guarantees good drainage. The ideal medium for sowing seed is a mixture of two parts sterilized garden soil, one part peat, and one part sand; add lime and a balanced fertilizer in minute quantities. Shop-bought seed compost or one of the proprietary peat-based composts are convenient and ready-prepared. Certain seeds with very hard seed coat (e.g. freesias) should be soaked in water for 24 hours prior to planting. As a rule, the smallest seeds can be sprinkled over the seed compost, but the larger ones need to be covered with a layer of compost or sand equal to their diameter. Water well with a watering can with a very fine spray. If the seeds are small it is better to stand the container in a bowl of water and let the moisture seep through slowly. One essential point is that the seeds should, as far as possible, be kept constantly moist. This can be done by covering the pot or seed tray with saran wrap (clingfilm) or glass, both of which should be removed when the seeds germinate. Germination may occur within anything from a few days to several weeks. In the case of *Lilium auratum* it may take up to three months. The ideal temperature, usually, is 57°–65°F (14°–18°C). When the seedlings are big enough to be handled conveniently, lift them from the compost with a spatula or small stick and replant them in potting compost 1¼–2 in (3–5 cm) apart. Take care not to damage the roots or stems. Then, depending on the species, you can keep them under glass for some time longer, and transfer them to a nursery bed in the garden to be grown in for a year or two.

Vegetative propagation. This is the method most often used for multiplying bulbous plants that are, as we have said, identical to the mother plant.

Bulbs and corms, when well developed, normally form small bulbs or corms around their base. When separated, these are able to lead an independent life and produce (generally within 2–3 years) new plants. The small bulbs or corms should be collected in the autumn, kept over the winter in a dry place and replanted in the spring, usually under glass so they can be cared for until they reach the necessary size for flowering. Gladioli produce many pea-sized cormels at the base of the corm. These are generally planted outdoors in the spring in furrows 12 in (30 cm) apart and 3–4 in (5–8 cm) deep, between two layers of sand and potting soil. They will flower after 2–3 years. Many lilies produce two or more bulbs that can be separated in autumn or spring. Tulips generally form bulblets of three sizes – large, medium and small. The smallest ones should be planted 2 in (5 cm) deep and the larger ones at a depth of 6 in (15 cm). The distance between them should be equal to double the size. The large ones flower after a year; the smaller, after 3 years.

Several species of *Lilium*, including *L. bulbiferum*, *L. tigrinum* and *L. sargentiae*, produce small purple-black or green bulbils in the leaf axils. These can be detached in August–September, when the leaves start to

The seedlings are transplanted into a container filled with potting compost. Dwarf dahlias (illustrated) sown in February–March, flower in the same year, unlike bulbous plants that are propagated by seed, which will only flower after 4–5 years.

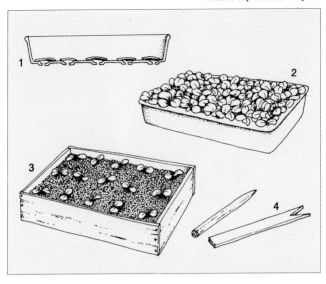

Freesia x kewensis. Freesia seeds have a hard outer casing and should therefore be soaked for 24 hours prior to planting.

turn yellow, and planted in rows in the nursery bed or in pots. Within one or, at most, a couple of years, they will be big enough to be planted out and to flower.

Certain ornamental species produce umbels of numerous aerial bulbils that can be treated in the same way as those of lilies.

Some Iridaceae, including gladioli and crocuses, can also be multiplied by division of the corms. In these cases the storage organs have to be cut vertically with a very sharp knife, taking care that each of the two portions has at least one bud and a piece of basal disk. The bared surfaces should then be sprinkled with a fungicide and, when dry, replanted.

The species with tubers and rhizomes can be propagated by simply dividing their subterranean organs, making certain that each piece retains at least one or two buds. This can be done for the rhizomes of callas, flowering cannas, rhizomatous iris, *Hedichium*, *Smithiantha*, etc., and the tubers of *Sinningia*, *Gloriosa*, etc.

Dividing the tuberous roots of dahlias is rather more complicated. These have buds only on the collar and must therefore be cut up in such a way that each new portion contains at least a piece of stem from the mother plant. It is always a good idea to complete the operation with a treatment of fungicidal dust that will prevent rot and fungal infections.

All species and hybrids of lilies may also be propagated by dividing the scales on the bulbs. In autumn or spring detach these carefully, leaving a small piece of the basal plate attached to each scale, and plant them at an angle, only half-way deep, in boxes filled with a sterile mixture of equal parts peat and sand (or you could use vermiculite). Small new bulbs will soon form at the base of the scales. The ideal temperature for success in this operation is 50°–54°F (10°–12°C). Watering should be gradually increased as the roots and bulblets develop.

Dahlias and tuberous begonias can also be multiplied by cuttings of shoots. This relatively simple technique makes it possible to obtain many new plants in a short time. Place tubers or tuberous roots in moist peat, wait for the formation of shoots and, when these are about 3 in (7–8 cm) long, separate them and root them in pots or boxes filled with a mixture of garden soil, peat and sand in equal parts, or a multi-purpose compost.

Some plants belonging to the family Gesneriaceae (*Sinningia, Smithiantha*, etc.) can be propagated by leaf cuttings. In May–June remove the leaves with stalks, set them in a mixture of peat and sand, and keep them at temperature of 68°–75°F (20°–24°C). Very soon new plantlets will appear, which should then be potted up in a good potting compost.

BULBOUS PLANTS INDOORS

Christmas-flowering potted plants. Some varieties (hyacinths, tulips, daffodils) can be especially prepared for forcing or early flowering indoors during the winter. The method consists basically of controlling temperature, light and humidity conditions artificially so as to alter and accelerate the natural life rhythms of the plants.

To achieve this result and to have plants flowering at home over Christmas or later in the winter, you must plant the bulbs in early autumn in containers in potting soil enriched with peat and sand (or proprietary peat-based compost or bulb fiber), either singly or in groups, with the tips just showing above the surface.

The bowls prepared in this way should be watered plentifully and placed in a dark, cold position at 39°–41°F (4°–5°C). Alternatively, you can put them in the garden inside a box with an outer protection of ashes, peat, and sand.

The initial forcing phase, which lasts 12–15 weeks, is intended to encourage the formation of the roots and the leaves. Throughout this first period all you need to do is make sure that the soil does not dry out. When the leaves measure 1¼–1½ in (3–4 cm), transfer the bowls into a cool, well-lit room at a temperature of around 50°F (10°C). After a further 10–15 days, when the leaves have reached a height of about 4 in (10 cm), the bowls or pots can finally be moved to their final indoor positions. Raise the temperature gradually to 65°F (18°C). They will soon flower. Thereafter, keep them at 54°–65°F (12°–18°C), away from any sources of heat, direct sunlight or drafts, and water plentifully and regularly.

To get staggered flowering, simply move the bowls from cold storage indoors at ten-day intervals.

As the flowers fade, cut off the stalks and move the bowls to a cooler place, at 39°–44°F (4°–7°C). Continue watering until you transplant the bulbs into the garden in March–April.

Bulbs grown in water. Some varieties of hyacinth and Tazetta narcissi

Vegetative reproductijon by division of tuberous roots e.g. dahlias (1); elongated rhizomes e.g. rhizomatous iris (2); bulbets that form at the base of the corms (3) and the bulbs (4); scales e.g. lilies (5). Opposite: two varieties of Dahlia x cultorum.

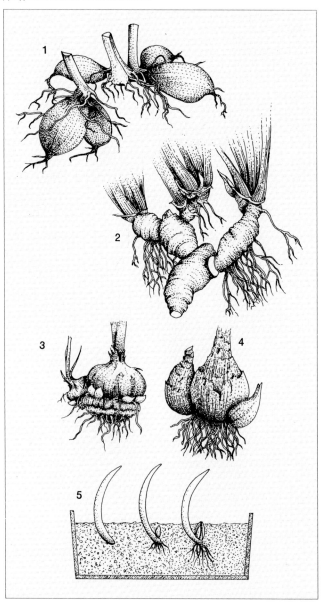

are peculiar in that they grow successfully in containers filled with water. Individual hyacinth bulbs are usually grown in special hyacinth glasses that are designed to hold the bulbs above water. Fill the wide base of the glass with water up to the base of the bulb. Then put the bulb for 4–5 weeks in a cool place indoors, dark in the case of hyacinths, light for daffodils, and when the roots are 3–4 in (7–10 cm) long and the leaves are beginning to sprout, move them to a warmer position where they will soon flower.

Small groups of narcissus bulbs are grown in large, fairly shallow bowls filled with pebbles. The bulbs are set on the pebbles and more pebbles are filled in around them, to anchor them, to a depth of about ³/₄ in (19 cm). Then pour in water to the surface of the pebbles and keep it at this level until flowering ends. Move the bulbs from a cool spot to their final blooming spot as above. Unfortunately, bulbs that are grown in water should be discarded after flowering.

Tender bulbs. Many delicate species, often tropical in origin, that must be planted outdoors in spring to flower in summer, can also be grown in the greenhouse or indoors and induced to flower early. Among these, perhaps the most common and popular are the *Hippeastrum* species, incorrectly called amaryllis. Planted at intervals from October to March, they will flower all winter. The large bulbs should be planted separately, only half covered, in pots of 5–6 in (12–15 cm) in diameter, in a mixture of one part peat, one part sand and one part potting compost, with an addition of natural ground limestone. (Any proprietary potting compost will do equally well.) Water moderately when potting and after the shoot appears. Feed fortnightly with liquid fertilizer throughout the growth period. Avoid a position in full sun. The leaves last longer than the flowers and should not be left without water.

Many other species can be treated in just the same way. They include, in particular, *Lachenalia*, *Vallotta*, *Nerine*, *Sprekelia*, etc. The bulbs should be planted with the tips just above the level of the soil. Except for freesias and *Lachenalia*, they can remain in the same pots for two years, *Vallotta* and *Nerine* can remain even longer. For more precise information see individual entries.

PESTS AND DISEASES OF BULBOUS PLANTS

Bulbous plants, like all living organisms, are subject to attack by numerous pests and diseases, principally insects, mites, nematodes, slugs and snails, and plant parasites that include diseases of fungal origin, bacteria and viruses. There are also physiological problems, not caused by pests or diseases.

PESTS

Aphids. Aphids are insects belonging to the order Hemiptera. They live in large colonies and attack a wide variety of plants, extracting sap with their piercing-sucking mouthparts. Depending on the species, they may cause bud damage, leaf shriveling or, in some cases, gall formation. They also spread viruses and emit honeydew, a sugary liquid on which some molds develop.

Control. In cases of initial attack, apply active insecticides which work on contact, or those based on pyrethrum. Against later infestations it is necessary to use systemic products that are carried throughout the plant, such as dimethoate. There are many good insecticides effective against aphids.

Greenhouse whitefly (*Trialeurodes vaporariorum*). This tropical fly, which resembles a tiny white moth, occurs frequently in greenhouses and in houseplants and sucks the sap from a great number of plants.

Control. Apply a dimethoate-based product.

Lily beetle (*Lilioceris lilii*). The scarlet-red beetle has reddish-yellow larvae that gnaw lilies, lilies of the valley, and fritillaries. It hibernates in the adult state.

Control. Treat with carbaryl-based products.

Click beetles. These are beetle larvae with a characteristic elongated, cylindrical shape, and a tough, yellowish tegument. (They are popularly known in Britain as wireworms.) They live in the soil and can damage bulbs and tubers by digging galleries inside them.

Control. As a rule they are a problem only in newly planned gardens. They can be got rid of by drainage, frequently turning over the ground or by applying an appropriate soil insecticide.

Swift moth (*Hepiolus humidi*). The larvae of this moth, $3/4–1/2$ in (2–4 cm) long, white with a dark head, dig galleries in the roots of many plants and attack particularly lilies of the valley and *Alstroemeria*.

Control. Basically by turning over the soil at regular intervals.

Water-lily beetle (*Galerucella nymphaeae*). The larvae of this beetle make long holes in the leaves of water-lilies (*Nymphaea* and *Nuphar*).

Control. Basically by mechanical elimination of the larvae. Try hosing them off the leaves for the fish to eat.

Snails and slugs. Polyphagous and nocturnal, snails belonging to the genus *Helix*, with coiled shells, and slugs of the genus *Limax*, without shells, will uninterruptedly devour the softest tissues of the aerial parts of plants, especially in wet weather and at night. Although unselective, they are particularly fond of lilies and dahlias. Unmistakable signs of their presence are traces of silvery slime left in their path.

Control. Set methaldehyde-based pellets close to the plants that need protection. It is also said that these pests love beer and will drown themselves in a saucer filled with the brew.

Above, from left to right: stages in the development of a hyacinth grown over water, to induce a "forced" flowering. Below, from left to right and top to bottom: the development of an amaryllis grown in a pot to induce early flowering.

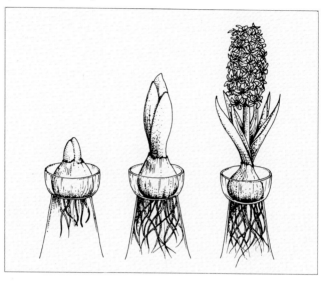

Narcissus bulb fly (*Eumerus strigatus*). The adult of this fly lays eggs on the collar of bulbous plants. The hatched larvae attack the underground organs and dig galleries in bulbs, corms, tubers or rhizomes of many ornamental plants, including lilies, iris, gladioli, daffodils and narcissi, hyacinths, etc.

Control. It is best to burn all infested bulbs or to plant healthy ones in a different area.

Nematodes. These microscopically small worms may live inside a large number of plants, causing swelling of roots and deformation of stems and leaves. One of the most widespread species is *Ditylencus dipsaci*, known as bulb and stem eelworms. They attack different bulbous plants, especially daffodils and hyacinths, causing black spots inside the bulbs, shriveling of flowers and leaves. There is also a root eelworm that mainly attacks the root system of cyclamens and begonias.

Control. Chemicals used by commercial growers are generally too toxic for amateurs to use. It is best to burn affected plants and replant fresh, healthy bulbs in another area.

Red spider mites. These minute creatures, the size of a pinhead, are mites belonging to the family Arachnidae. They have piercing-sucking mouthparts, with which they repeatedly pierce the leaves of many plants, extracting the sap. They do extensive damage because they multiply so rapidly.

Control. Basically by using acaricides.

Mice. Mice seem to be particularly fond of bulbs, corms, and tubers, which they devour freely. Crocuses are especially appetizing.

Control. In the garden the best protection is by means of poison baits. Also, eliminate molehills which mice use as tunnels. (Moles themselves do not eat bulbs.)

Thrips. These small insects, belonging to the order Thysanoptera, use their piercing-sucking mouthparts to extract sap from the leaves and petals, causing silvery spots, deformations, flower drop and arrested leaf development. The greenhouse thrip (*Heliothrips haemorrhoidalis*) attacks various plants grown under glass, while the gladiolus thrip (*Thaeniothrips simplex*, syn. *Thrips simplex*) infests the corms, leaves and flowers of gladioli, causing silvery spots or deformations. It hibernates in the corms, turning them black and sticky.

Control. Use a constant insecticide, such as malathion, on growing plants; dust corms before storing or planting with a gamma-HCH dust. For gladioli, simply make sure the corms are healthy, but they can be disinfected by soaking in water at 113°F (45°C) for 30 minutes.

PLANT PARASITES

Cyclamen anthracnose (*Gloeosporium cyclaminis*). This is widespread in greenhouse cultivation and causes rotting of new buds on the tubers, while the stalks, and sometimes the leaves and the flowers, are covered with flat oval blotches.

Control. You could try treating with a fungicide, but it may be best to destroy the affected plant.

Bacteria. There are several species of bacteria that attack bulbous plants, including gladioli (*Pseudomonas marginalis*) and hyacinths (*P. hyacinthi*), causing leaf spotting and bulb rot respectively.

Control. Destroy affected plants and do not grow bulbs there again for as long as possible.

Bulb gangrene (*Sclerotinia gladioli*). This fungus attacks the leaves of crocuses and gladioli, causing them to turn yellow and to wither. Corms exhibit large black rotting growths.

Control. Destroy sick plants and shift to another site.

Fusarium wilt. This term is used for a series of diseases caused by fungi belonging to the genus *Fusarium*, most common in hot, wet climates and in acid, badly drained soil. It may affect many species including crocuses, gladioli, lilies, daffodils, etc. The usual consequences are rotting of bulbs or corms and shriveling of the plants.

Control. The main safeguards are to use healthy plants, to select resistant varieties and to improve the soil.

Sclerosis (*Sclerotinia tuliparum*). This is a disease caused by a fungus that mainly attacks tulips and hyacinths. It attacks the bulbs, producing a gray mold and destroying tissue.

Control. Destroy all sick plants and replant healthy bulbs elsewhere. Soaking the bulbs in benomyl or thiophanate-methyl may help control an early infestation.

Soft rot. This is caused by various fungi (*Sclerotinia sclerotiorum*, *Botrytis gladiolorum*) that attack the internal tissues of hyacinth bulbs, *Acidanthera* corms and the tuberous roots of dahlias while they are being stored, first turning them black and then rotten.

Control. Keep bulbs, corms and roots in cool, airy places.

Gladiolus dry rot (*Stromatinia gladioli*). This fungus attacks gladioli, crocuses, freesias and *Acidanthera*, producing tiny black spots aroundthe collar. The leaves turn yellow and wither, and the underground organs are damaged.

Control. Destroy affected plants. Use healthy bulbs and corms.

Gray mold (*Botrytis cinereas*). Attacks of gray mold, which produce spots on the leaves, flowers, and bulbs, are particularly severe in damp, rainy periods. If the attack is violent, the affected parts are covered with

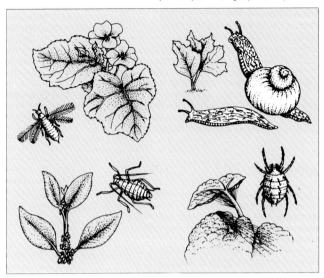

a continuous thick layer of mold. Among the many plants infested are tulips, gladioli and hyacinths.

Control. Use healthy plant material, without lesions, and if necessary treat with copper-based products, or benomyl or thiophanate-methyl.

Penicillum. These are fungi, belonging to various species, responsible for the appearance of green or blue-green molds while bulbs, corms, and tubers are being stored.

Control. Plant material should be stored in cool, dry places. Affected plants should be destroyed and, as a preventive measure, other healthy bulbs or corms dipped in benomyl or thiophanate-methyl for 15–30 minutes before planting or storing.

Rust. Various species of fungi cause the appearance on numerous plants, including iris, of tiny reddish-brown pustules, single or in groups, on the leaves. Damage is generally limited.

Control. Use resistant plant varieties.

Septoriosis. This disease is caused by fungi belonging to the genus *Septoria*. It is especially troublesome in wet climates, and is serious in the greenhouse. It affects many plants, producing spots on the leaves. In gladioli it also affects the corms.

Control. As soon as the first symptoms appear, treat with copper-based products.

Virus diseases. The extremely small, non-cellular organisms known as viruses cause several serious diseases. They produce green or yellow spots or streaks, blotches of discoloration, dwarfism of plants and, in some instances, leaf swellings, blisters and other abnormal growths. Viruses may attack crocuses, dahlias, gladioli, iris, lilies and freesias. In the case of tulips, a virus is responsible for characteristic color contrasts that are highly prized (Rembrandt tulips).

Control. Viruses are transmitted from one plant to another by aphids and other insects with piercing-sucking mouthparts. So treatment must be directed against the carriers, as already indicated. Destroy affected plants if the virus is one that affects plant growth.

PHYSIOLOGICAL

Chlorosis. Leaves attacked by chlorosis first turn yellowish, then shrivel at the edges and drop off. The phenomenon is due to the inadequate formation or destruction of chlorophyll and must be considered in the context of soil nutrients, particularly lack of iron, and is often induced by a high pH (a very alkaline soil).

Control. Apply iron chelates directly to the soil and as a foliar feed. Follow the manufacturer's instructions.

Damage from cold. This may occur as a result of low temperatures, usually in spring or autumn, following a late or early frost. The buds turn brown and spots appear on the leaves.

Etiolation. This mainly affects house and greenhouse plants when there is insufficient light. The shoots are pale, thin, and elongated.

A note on zones (U.S.A.)

In the plant entries we have given the coldest climate zone in which each plant can be safely grown. This map is reproduced opposite. The zone numbers mean that if you live in zone 6, for example, you can safely plant outdoors any bulb that grows in zones 1–6; you can, however, only grow bulbs listed for zones 7–10 if you plant them in pots or dig them up from the garden and bring them indoors over winter. Tender bulbs that cannot be grown outdoors the year round even in zone 10 are listed in the entries as "tender."

Most the the British Isles would fall in zone 8, with the exception of coastal areas in southern and western England, Wales and Scotland and all but the eastern coast of Ireland, which would be in zone 9.

ZONES OF PLANT HARDINESS

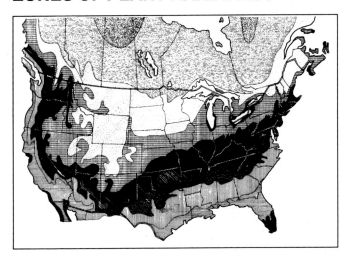

Approximate range of average annual minimum temperatures for each zone.

⬤ Zone 1 Below −50°F (−45°C)

◉ Zone 2 −50°F to −35°F (−45°C to −37°C)

◯ Zone 3 −35°F to −20°F (−37°C to −28°C)

◍ Zone 4 −20°F to −10°F (−28°C to −23°C)

● Zone 5 −10°F to −5°F (−23°C to −20.5°C)

● Zone 6 −5°F to 5°F (−20.5°C to −15°C)

● Zone 7 5°F to 10°F (−15°C to −12°C)

◍ Zone 8 10°F to 20°F (−12°C to −6.5°C)

◉ Zone 9 20°F to 30°F (−6.5°C to −1°C)

● Zone 10 30°F to 40°F (−1°C to −4.5°C)

1 ACHIMENES LONGIFLORA

Family Gesneriaceae.
Origin Tropical central and southern America.
Description Tender, herbaceous perennial, with a distinctive scaly rootstock of catkin-like tubers; ovate hairy leaves, coarsely serrated and grouped in whorls of three. Flowers trumpet-shaped, five-petaled, orange or scarlet, measuring about 2 in (5 cm) across.
Flowering period July to September.
Cultivation Can be cultivated as a house plant or in the greenhouse. Requires high temperatures and humidity, until it produces the flowers, after which it can be moved into the house for display; it is thus really a greenhouse plant. To start into growth: ideal temperature 61°–65°F (16°–18°C). Plant tubers February–April, preferably in peaty soil, in pots or baskets, about 1¹/₄ in (3 cm) apart and covered with ³/₄ in (2 cm) of soil. Water moderately at first, then freely when the plant is in full growth. Feed with liquid fertilizer every fortnight. Shade from fierce sunlight, and spray-mist early or late in the day.
Propagation From seed in March, bud or leaf cuttings in April, or by division of young tubers during the rest period, in February.
Care Once the foliage has died down in autumn, pots should be placed on their sides in the greenhouse, where the rootstock can ripen, protected from frost until spring.
Other species *A. grandiflora, A. heterophylla*, and many hybrids in a range of colors.

---

2 ACIDANTHERA BICOLOR c.v. MURIELAE
(now **GLADIOLUS CALLIANTHUS** c.v. **MURIELAE**)

Family Iridaceae.
Origin Eastern half of Africa (Ethiopia to Malawi).
Description Herbaceous plant up to 43 in (110 cm) tall in flower, with corm and few linear leaves. A graceful spike above leaves of sweetly-scented pure white flowers with a prominent central purple blotch.
Flowering period Late summer: September–October.
Cultivation Half-hardy, and cannot withstand frost. Corms may be planted in the open if well sheltered from cold and wind but must be lifted after flowering before the first frosts. Needs fertile, well-drained soil in full sun. Plant corms in pots in March–April, keep in greenhouse until frosts are over, then plant out in early May, about 4 in (10 cm) deep and about 8 in (20 cm) apart. Water frequently; feed with liquid fertilizer every 3–4 weeks. Leaves and stems may be damaged by slugs, leaves and flowers by aphids; corms are subject to rot, especially if drainage is poor or corms are overwatered.
Propagation Separate small corms in autumn.
Care Plants grown in the open must be lifted before the first frosts and gradually dried off in a cool house, and stored until spring. In pots, reduce watering as foliage dies down and keep pots dry until repotting in early spring.

3 AGAPANTHUS AFRICANUS

(Syn. **A. umbellatus, A. praecox**)   **U.S. zone 10**

African lily

Family Liliaceae.

Origin South Africa (Cape Province).

Description Like all the *Agapanthus*, this species has fleshy tuberous roots and will form a compact clump. The rich green strap-shaped ligulate leaves are normally evergreen. The pale, deep blue or blue-violet flowers, 2–3 in (5–8 cm) long, are borne in crowded umbels on tall stems 24–28 in (60–70 cm) high. *A africanus* subspecies *orientalis* has particularly rich blue flowers. There is also a double blue and single white form.

Flowering period July to early autumn.

Cultivation Withstands frost fairly well and in temperate zones can be grown outside. Likes sunny positions in deep, fertile, moist but well-drained soil. The tuberous rootstock should be planted out in April, with crowns about 2 in (5 cm) below soil level and left undisturbed. Plant 15–18 in (38–46 cm) apart. Pot specimens tend to outgrow containers, so repot every year.

Propagation From seed in the greenhouse or by division of crowns in spring.

Care In winter stems should be cut down to ground level and the crowns covered with leaves or straw. In cold climates grow in tubs in a sunny, sheltered position outside, but move to a frost-free greenhouse for winter.

---

4 AGAPANTHUS CAMPANULATUS

U.S. zone 10

Family Liliaceae.

Origin Southern Africa.

Description This deciduous species has many fleshy tuberous roots producing tufts of grayish-green linear leaves, about 24 in (60 cm) tall. The long, sturdy, rounded stem, 6–12 in (15–30 cm) across, bears beautiful umbellate, rather flat heads of flowers, composed of 10–30 or more funnel-shaped soft blue flowers. There is also a white form. The cultivar 'Isis' has lavender-blue flowers.

Flowering period Late summer.

Cultivation Can be planted outside only in temperate zones, otherwise best grown in pots. Reasonably tolerant of frost. Likes sunny positions in deep, fertile, well-drained soil. Crowns should be planted out in spring, about 2 in (5 cm) deep. Pot specimens tend to outgrow containers, so repot every two years.

Propagation From seed in greenhouse or by division of clumps in spring.

Care In winter stems should be cut down to ground level and crowns well-covered with leaves or straw. In cold climates keep plants in pots but remove to greenhouse for the winter months and keep fairly dry.

5 ALLIUM CAERULEUM
(Syn. *A. azureum*)

Family Liliaceae.
Origin Central Asia and Siberia.
Description Leaves triangular in section, mostly withered by flowering time, stem about 12–23in (30–60cm) tall, carrying a very tight umbel, 1¼–1½in (3–4cm) across, of many small blue flowers. Not an invasive species.
Flowering period May to July.
Cultivation Easy to grow in any sunny, well-drained soil. Plant bulbs in autumn or spring 4–6in (10–15cm) deep and 10in (25cm) apart. Water only during periods of prolonged drought.
Propagation By division of bulbs at end of growing season. Plants can also be raised from seed but require 2–3 years to flower.
Care Bulbs can remain in the ground, undisturbed for years. A winter covering of leaves is advisable only in very cold climates.

6 ALLIUM FLAVUM

Family Liliaceae.
Origin Southern and eastern Europe.
Description A very variable species 2–12in (5–30cm) tall. A small, rounded bulb with a light brown tunic, leaves narrow, cylindrical, gray-green and sheathing the lower half of the stem. Umbellate inflorescences 1½in (3–4cm) across, with pale to deep yellow flowers, bell-shaped, on long graceful stalks, the outer ones pendulous.
Flowering period Summer.
Cultivation Easy to grow, likes full sun, and a dry, sandy soil. Plant bulbs in autumn 4–6in (10–15cm) deep and 10in (25cm) apart. The very dwarf mountain forms are ideal for the rock garden. Some tall forms are particularly gray-leaved, others are sweetly scented.
Propagation By division of small clumps at end of growing season. Plants can also be raised from seed, but need 2–3 years to flower.
Care Bulbs will survive for years in the ground if the drainage is good. A winter covering of leaves is advisable only in coldest climates.

7 ALLIUM GIGANTEUM

Family Liliaceae.
Origin Central Asia.
Description Basal tuft of slightly glaucous, strap-shaped leaves, appearing early, 16–18 in (40–45 cm) long. Stout stem of 28–60 in (90–150 cm), terminating in a dense, spherical umbel, 4–6 in (10–15 cm) across, composed of small bright pink to lilac stellate flowers. Well-grown specimens may reach 78 in (200 cm) in height.
Flowering period Early to mid summer.
Cultivation Easy to grow, in full sun and any well-drained soil. Plant bulbs in autumn 4–6 in (10–15 cm) deep and 10 in (25 cm) apart. If happy, they will persist without trouble for years. Water only in periods of severe drought in spring.
Propagation By division of bulbs at end of growing season. Sow seeds in autumn in greenhouse and transplant seedlings into beds outside after one year. However, they need 3–4 years to flower.
Care A winter covering of leaves is advisable only in coldest climates. The old flower stems should be cut down in autumn.

8 ALLIUM MOLY

Family Liliaceae.
Origin Northwestern Mediterranean region.
Description Rounded bulb with white tunic, forming offsets freely. Gray-green lanceolate leaves, one to two per bulb $1^{1}/_{4} \times 6$–8 in (3 × 15–20 cm), clasping the flower stalk at its base. The 6–10 in (15–25 cm) rounded stems bear dome-shaped umbels, 2–3 in (5–7 cm) across, with large deep-yellow starry flowers, fading to whitish.
Flowering period Spring.
Cultivation Likes sun or half-shade and a slightly moist, well-drained soil. Plant bulbs in autumn 4–6 in (10–15 cm) deep and 10 in (25 cm) apart. Useful for naturalizing beneath deciduous trees and shrubs. May also be grown in pots in partial shade in a cool frame, but should be dried slightly after flowering.
Propagation By division of bulbs at end of growing season, but only after several years from time of planting out. Can also be raised from seed, sown in autumn or spring, but need 2–3 years to flower.
Care Bulbs can remain for years in the ground without problem. A winter covering of leaves is advisable only in coldest climates.

9 ALLIUM NARCISSIFLORUM
(Syn. *A. pedemontanum*)

Family Liliaceae.
Origin Northwest Portugal, southern France, and northern Italy.
Description Slender, elongated bulb with thick, fibrous tunic, forming rhizomatous clumps. Leaves linear $^3/_{16}$in (4mm) wide, or less, clasping the stem at the base. Stem 6–12in (15–30cm) tall, carrying a loose pendant umbel of 5–8 bell-like flowers, pinkish-purple, with long petals. *A. insubricum* from northern Italy is more commonly cultivated. It is closely related (but not as handsome) with broader leaves, fewer, longer flowers and papery bulb coats.
Flowering period July–August.
Cultivation A hardy plant requiring a position in full sun with well-drained soil. Since it is very susceptible to wet winter conditions it is more suitable for a sunny, free-draining slope in the rock garden. Plant bulbs in autumn 4–6in (10–15cm) deep and 10in (25cm) apart.
Propagation By division of clumps at end of growing season. Plants can also be raised from seed but will take 2–3 years to flower.
Care The bulbs can normally stay in the ground but dislike excessive winter wet. A covering of leaves in winter is advisable only in the coldest climates.

---

10 ALLIUM NEAPOLITANUM

Family Liliaceae.
Origin Mediterranean region.
Description Plant 8–16in (20–40cm) tall, bulb with white tunic and numerous reddish bulbils. Few leaves, linear-lanceolate, sheathing the lower part of the stem. Loose umbel, of 2$^1/_2$–3$^1/_2$in (6–9cm) in diameter, composed of numerous large pure white, sweet-smelling flowers.
Flowering period Early spring. Flowering may be earlier in greenhouse.
Cultivation One of the least hardy of all alliums, so best grown in containers that can be given frost protection in winter. There is a good demand for the pleasantly scented cut flowers. It needs a position in full sun in normal soil. Plant bulbs in early autumn 4–6in (10–15cm) deep. Apply liquid fertilizer in the spring. Water moderately.
Propagation By detaching bulbils at end of growing season, or from seed.
Care Since the species is not very hardy, it is best grown in pots with greenhouse protection in winter.

11 ALLIUM SCHOENOPRASUM
Chives

Family Liliaceae.
Origin Alpine and cool–temperate zones of Europe, Asia and North America.
Description Bulb narrowly bottle-shaped, eventually forming dense tufts. Cylindrical leaves 10–14 in (25–35 cm) long and ¼ in (2–4 mm) across, and sheaths enfolding the first third of the stem. Umbel compact, egg-shaped or hemispherical, 1½ in (3–4 cm) across, composed of numerous pale lilac or purple, occasionally white, flowers.
Flowering period Late spring–summer.
Cultivation The species is very variable in the wild and many forms are commonly grown in the herb garden since the chopped-up leaves are used in cooking. It is a hardy plant, suitable for a position in sun or partial shade, in medium soil. Water freely in dry weather. Plant bulbs in autumn 4–6 in (10–15 cm) deep. Kept in pots, in a sheltered place, chives will grow through the winter. Apply manure in winter or early spring.
Propagation By division of clumps in autumn.
Care Clumps are best lifted and divided every four years and replanted in fresh ground. Outside clumps protected by cloches during the winter will produce much earlier leaves for culinary use.

12 ALLIUM URSINUM
"Ramsons"

Family Liliaceae.
Origin Europe and eastward to Russia.
Description Soft bulb with whitish tunic. Elliptical leaves measuring 1½–2½ × 5–6 in (4–6 × 12–16 cm), basal, with long stalks and a slightly hairy surface. The stalk is 8–14 in (20–35 cm) semi-cylindrical and terminates in a 1–2½ in (3–6 cm) umbel composed of numerous white, flat starry flowers.
Flowering period Late spring to early summer.
Cultivation Very invasive. Should be confined to naturalizing in woods. Prefers a sheltered, semi-shaded position in fertile soil. Plant bulbs in autumn or spring 4–6 in (10–15 cm) deep and 10 in (25 cm) apart. Abundant watering unnecessary.
Propagation By division of clumps in autumn. Plants can also be raised from seed, but need 2–3 years to flower.
Care Bulbs can be left in the ground without problem, but may take over large areas if left unchecked.

13 ALSTROEMERIA AURANTIACA

U.S. zone 6

Family Alstroemeriaceae (formerly Amaryllidaceae).
Origin Chile.
Description Perennial herbaceous plant up to 3 ft (1 m) tall, with thick, fleshy, running roots. Erect, wiry stems bear light green narrow leaves and heads of small lily-flowers. These are funnel-shaped, about 2 in (5 cm) across, rich yellow to orange-scarlet, with red veining on the two upper petals.
Flowering period Summer.
Cultivation A hardy plant which needs a temperate climate and must not be subjected to standing water in winter. In cold regions it grows best in full sun, but in warm areas it will thrive in partial shade. Soil must be rich and, above all, well-drained. Plant roots in autumn or potted seedlings in early spring, 9 in (23 cm) deep, in sheltered spots. Support young and fragile stems with twigs (or brushwood) to prevent them from breaking. During the first season the plant may grow poorly because the root system is highly sensitive to transplanting and needs time to establish itself. Feed in autumn with well-rotted manure. Likely to be attacked by slugs and snails and viruses transmitted by aphids.
Propagation By division of roots in early autumn, taking great care not to damage them, or from seed in March in a cold greenhouse for planting out the following season, or by seed sown in situ.
Care Cut stems to ground-level in late summer and protect rootstock with a generous layer of straw or bracken. In particularly cold or wet climates grow plants in containers and bring them in for the winter.
Other species *A. chilensis*, *A. ligtu*, *A. pelegrina*, *A pulchella*, *A. violacea*.

14 AMARYLLIS BELLADONNA

(Syn. ***Hippeastrum equestre, Callicore rosea***) **U.S. zone 5**
Belladonna lily

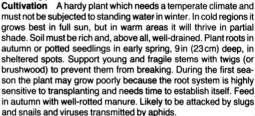

Family Amaryllidaceae.
Origin Southern Africa.
Description Plant with large, pear-shaped bulb, and 4–8 strap-shaped, glossy leaves, 8–20 in (20–50 cm) long, in a fan-like basal tuft. The stout stem terminates in an umbel of large, trumpet-shaped, pink or white, scented flowers, each about 3 in (8 cm) across. The flowers appear in late summer before the leaves, which grow from late autumn to early summer. The plant is poisonous. 'Hathor' has white flowers with a yellow throat, 'Parkeri' pink flowers with a yellow throat.
Flowering period Late summer, autumn.
Cultivation To flower well, this plant prefers a warm, temperate climate. In Britain, a hot, sunny position is essential. Grows well in rich, deep and well-drained soil. Plant bulbs in late summer directly in ground, 8 in (20 cm) deep. Make sure that the tips of the bulbs show. Water freely in dry weather until leaves start to yellow; water again in late summer as flower stems appear. Annual top dressing of bonemeal in late summer or well-rotted manure in spring.
Propagation From division of established clumps as leaves turn yellow in early summer.
Care In winter a light covering of bracken or a pane of glass above the leaves will give some protection against frost.

15 ANEMONE APENNINA

Family Ranunculaceae.
Origin Southeastern Europe, especially in Carpathian–Danube region.
Description Species 4–14 in (10–35 cm) tall, with blackish tuberous rhizome. Upright, fragile flower stem, reddened at base, with leafy bracts in whorls of three; basal leaves with long stalk and triangular blade divided into three coarsely-toothed palmate segments. Single flowers 1½ in (3–4 cm) across, generally blue, sometimes white. 'Plena' and 'Purpurea' both have double flowers.
Flowering period Spring.

Cultivation This hardy species dislikes hot, very dry conditions. Grows well in light shade of trees and in grass, and is particularly suitable for rock gardens, especially partially shaded sites. Does well in both acid and alkaline soils, provided they are cool and well-drained. Rhizomes can be planted out in September, 4–6 in (10–15 cm) apart and covered with 2 in (5 cm) of soil. Top dress every autumn with well-decayed leafmold.
Propagation By division of rhizomes in autumn and from seed in sandy soil in cold greenhouse, although plantlets need two years before they flower.
Care Will naturalize and form extensive colonies beneath trees. Can be invasive where happy and is ideal for a wild garden. Flowers for arrangement should always be cut, never pulled, or rhizomes are likely to be tugged out of the ground.

16 ANEMONE BLANDA

Family Ranunculaceae.
Origin Eastern Mediterranean.
Description Plant about 6 in (15 cm) tall, with dark, knobbly tuber, leaves roughly circular in outline divided into biternate segments, and daisy-like flowers 1½–2 in (4–5 cm) across, light blue, pink, lavender or white according to selected variety.
Flowering period February–April.

Cultivation Hardy, highly adaptable species, not very sensitive to frost. Grows well in moist but well-drained soil, acid or alkaline, in sun or half-shade. Particularly suitable for a cool corner in the rock garden. Rhizomes should be planted out in September, while still dormant. Cover with 2 in (5 cm) of soil and set 4 in (10 cm) apart. Apply manure in autumn.

Propagation By division of tubers in autumn or from seed in cold greenhouse; in the latter case, seedlings can be planted out after a couple of years.
Care Suitable for naturalizing beneath deciduous trees and shrubs, or in grass. The only precaution against damaging them is always to cut flowers with a knife or secateurs (shears); do not pull at the stems.

17 ANEMONE CORONARIA
Poppy anemone

Family Ranunculaceae.
Origin Mediterranean region.
Description Species 6–12 in (15–30 cm) tall, with flattened compact tuber, upright, thick, flexible stem, basal leaves biternate and finely cut, stem leaves forming a frilly collar just below the flowers. These are white, blue, red, single or double, depending on variety.
Flowering period If planted at intervals, flowering is continuous.
Cultivation This needs a warmer and sunnier climate than many other anemone species. It will not survive long in cold regions. Must have good drainage and full sun. Plant tubers at intervals from end of September to April in order to have a succession of flowering plants. Soak rootstocks in water for one night before planting out, then set about 6 in (15 cm) apart. In Britain, for winter-flowering, protect with cloches from October.
Propagation From seed, in late autumn, in cold greenhouse. Young stock can be planted out after one year.
Care Tubers quickly deteriorate and should be replaced every 2–3 years.

---

18 ANEMONE NEMOROSA
European wood anemone

Family Ranunculaceae.
Origin Cold and cool–temperate areas of Europe and western Asia.
Description Slender brown rhizome, basal leaves with long stalk and blade divided into three deeply lobed segments, stem leaves smaller and in whorls of three. The single white flower is 1 in (2.5 cm) across, usually with 6–7 narrowly elliptical petals, pink or purple tinged beneath. Cultivated varieties usually have bigger flowers. 'Robinsoniana' has lavender-blue flowers, grayish outside. Selected double forms are also available.
Flowering period February–April.
Cultivation In the wild often favors deciduous woods, especially those of oak and beech – forming thick carpets of flowers when winter is over. Likes shady positions and fertile, well-drained soil. Plant rhizomes 6 in (15 cm) apart in autumn and top dress with fresh leafmold.
Propagation By division of rhizomes in autumn for selected forms, or from seed.
Care Ideal for naturalizing beneath deciduous trees and shrubs or for the wild garden. Can eventually become invasive.

19 ANTHERICUM LILIAGO
St Bernard's lily

Family Liliaceae.
Origin Western Europe and Mediterranean coasts.
Description Hairless herbaceous perennial 1–2 ft (30–60 cm) tall, with an unbranched stem, a basal tuft of gray-green grassy leaves 1/8–3/8 in (3–8 mm) wide, and loose raceme of 10–30 starry flowers 1–1 1/2 in (2–4 cm) across, with white petals and curved style. Rootstock a short rhizome with long, wiry, slightly fleshy roots; clump-forming.
Flowering period May–June.
Cultivation Grows in the wild, in dry meadows, open woods and on sunny hillsides. It is not difficult to cultivate. Grows well in sun or very light shade, very suitable for rock gardens and the herbaceous border. Plant in autumn 4 in (10 cm) deep. Often does not flower the first year because the extensive root system needs time to get established. Feed in spring when leaves appear.
Propagation In autumn or spring, by division of established clumps only. Seeds can also be sown in spring, but 2–3 years are needed before the plants flower.
Care Clumps are best left undisturbed for some years, and a winter covering of leaves or straw applied in colder climates.
Other species *A. ramosum.*

---

20 ARISAEMA CANDIDISSIMUM

Family Araceae.
Origin Western China.
Description Very beautiful, deciduous aroid with rounded, flattened tuber. The "flower", held on a 6-in (15-cm) stem, is a white tubular spathe, 3–4 in (8–10 cm), with an expanded hood, pinkish vertical striping in the throat, and often a pinkish or greenish suffusion outside. Concealed within the tube, and protected by the pointed hood, is the spadix – a pencil-like white or yellowish column bearing the tiny true flowers in a broad band. Male and female flowers are borne on separate plants. The pair of large, bold leaves are three-lobed and expand after flowering to about 12 in (30 cm) in height.
Flowering period June.
Cultivation The ideal situation for this very hardy adaptable woodlander is a rich, moist soil in sun or part-shade. It particularly dislikes hot, dry summers. Plant late summer to early autumn, about 3–4 in (7–10 cm) deep. When happy, it will produce offsets and form clumps.
Propagation By offset tubers in late summer or fresh seed in autumn, sown under glass.
Care Top dress with leafmold or well-rotted manure in autumn. As growth does not appear above ground until June, mark the position of planted tubers to avoid damaging them during cultivation.

21 ARISARUM PROBOSCIDEUM
Mousetail plant

Family Araceae.
Origin Central and southern Italy.
Description Plant 1–1½ in (2–4 cm) tall, sometimes 4 in (10 cm) or even taller. Leaf with long stalk and sagittate blade. Small flowers grouped in a 1-in (2-cm) olive-purple spadix, club-shaped at tip, completely enclosed by a brownish spathe which is extended into a curved, tail-like appendage, 3–6 in (8–15 cm). The inflorescences look like mice with long tails half-hidden among the foliage.
Flowering period April–May.
Cultivation Hardy plant that likes wet woods and clearings. Grows well in cool soil, rich in humus and peat, in a partially shaded position. Too much sun may harm it. Adapts to pot cultivation in a shady corner of balcony or patio. Plant rhizomes 6 in (15 cm) deep in autumn or spring.
Propagation By division of rhizomes in early spring when plant is already well established.
Care Rhizomes should be left in ground during winter and protected with a layer of leaves in colder climates.

---

22 ARUM ITALICUM

Family Araceae.
Origin Mainly Mediterranean coasts.
Description Plant 16–20 in (40–50 cm) tall, with oval tuber. The leaves, with a spear-shaped blade, generally have white veining or marking, and in temperate climates grow in autumn through winter until the following spring. The yellow spathe envelops the club-shaped spadix. The fruits are highly decorative but poisonous red berries that ripen in autumn.
Flowering period March–May.
Cultivation Widespread Mediterranean species in deciduous woods, clearings and hedgerows. Likes semi-shade and cool, fertile, well-drained soil. Too much damp may damage root system. Plant tubers 3 in (7 cm) deep in early spring or late summer.
Propagation By division of tubers in late summer. Self-sown seedlings may appear.
Care Tubers can be kept in the ground without problem. Avoid standing water that can cause root rot.

23 ASPHODELUS ALBUS
Asphodel

Family Liliaceae.
Origin Mediterranean mountain regions, southern Europe.
Description Although not a bulbous plant in the true sense, this possesses fleshy roots that are as thick as tubers. These underground organs have the peculiarity of not being harmed by fire; hence asphodels commonly grow wild in areas frequently subject to fires, and despite the delightful sight of them flowering in spring, they are a sign of a deteriorating environment. They are about 3 ft (1 m) tall, with an erect, glabrous stem, upright linear basal leaves, and white-petaled flowers with a central green vein. The flowers are 1¹/₂ in (4 cm) across and grow in dense terminal racemes.
Flowering period May–June.
Cultivation Asphodels are hardy and extremely adaptable. They prefer sunny positions and sandy, well-drained soil. They tolerate drought well. Plant the roots in autumn and cover with 3 in (7–8 cm) of soil.
Propagation By division of roots during resting period, or from seed.
Care Roots can stay in the ground during winter without problem.
Other species *A. fistolosus*, *A. ramosus*. *A. leutens* (more correctly *Asphodeline lutea*) is the one more commonly grown in the U.K.

24 BABIANA STRICTA

Family Iridaceae.
Origin Southern Africa.
Description The name of this genus is said to have derived from the Afrikaans *bobbejaan* meaning "baboon," because these animals are very fond of the corms. The plant is 6–12 in (15–30 cm) tall, with lance-shaped, rough, pleated leaves. The flowers are upright, funnel-shaped, 1 in (2.5 cm) across, in dense spikes. Colors range from blue to pink, crimson or violet, according to variety.
Flowering period Spring.
Cultivation A rather delicate species that needs a sheltered, warm position in full sun and fertile soil rich in organic matter. It can be grown in the open only in temperate climates but is not resistant to frost. Plant corms in spring 6 in (15 cm) deep. The plant is also suitable for small beds and rock gardens and for pot cultivation indoors. To obtain winter flowers, pot in autumn, water and feed monthly at the beginning of plant growth until time of flowering.
Propagation By division of corms during rest period or from seed in greenhouse in spring.
Care In warm climates the corms can be left in the ground throughout the winter, but in temperate areas should be protected with a 6-in (15-cm) layer of leaves and straw. In colder climates they are best lifted in autumn, stored in a cool, frost-proof place, and replanted in spring.

25 BEGONIA × TUBERHYBRIDA

Tuberous-rooted begonia **tender**

Family Begoniaceae.
Origin Cultivated hybrids.
Description The group comprises numerous hybrid tuberous begonias of complex derivation, and are variable in habit, size and color. They are very popular flowering plants, up to 24 in (60 cm) tall, and bushy plants can be up to 18 in (45 cm) wide. The stems are short, reddish-green, and the leaves alternate, irregular, rough and fleshy. The flowers come in a wide range of colors except blue and mauve. Separate male and female flowers appear on the same plant.
Flowering period Summer and early autumn.
Cultivation The plants are suitable for flower beds, although they are not resistant to frost, and as potted plants in greenhouse, on patio or indoors. They need fertile soil that is rich in organic matter and given a feeding of manure; it must be well-drained, and in a sheltered position, in sun or partial shade. Plant tubers inside at 65°F (18°C) March–April, and place outside after a couple of months. Water plentifully and frequently. The plants are attacked by nematodes, mites, gray mold, root rot and bacteria. The pendulous types are best in hanging baskets or pots, and the really large-flowered varieties are best grown as pot plants or in a greenhouse.
Propagation By stem or young shoot cuttings. Seed of some varieties may also be sown indoors in January at 61°–65°F (16°–18°C) to obtain first flowers in early summer.
Care Lift tubers in late autumn, dry them in sheltered and temperate surroundings, clean and keep them in bags of peat at 39°–50°F (4°–10°C).

26 BELAMCANDA CHINENSIS

U.S. zone 5

Family Iridaceae.
Origin Asia, Japan.
Description Plant 28–36 in (70–90 cm) tall with tuberous roots, slender stems, pointed linear leaves, and numerous flowers, about 2 in (5 cm) wide, salmon-orange with red spots. These quickly fade but are continually renewed. They are followed by capsules that open in late summer to reveal groups of shiny black berries that can be used for floral displays.
Flowering period Summer.
Cultivation This half-hardy species grows well in warm, sunny spots, in sandy but fertile soil. It will not withstand severe frosts. It is also suitable for growing in pots that can be sheltered in winter. Plant tuberous roots in spring 6 in (15 cm) apart and cover with 1½ in (3–4 cm) of soil.
Propagation By division of tuberous roots in spring or from seed, again in spring, in greenhouse.
Care In autumn, when leaves fade, remove roots from ground and shelter from frost. Potted plants should also be placed under cover.

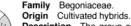

27 BELLEVALIA ROMANA
(Syn. *Hyacinthus romanus*)   U.S. zone 6

Family   Liliaceae.
Origin   Southern Europe, Mediterranean region.
Description   This small hyacinth, 8–10 in (20–25 cm) tall, has a bulb with a papery skin like a tulip, fleshy, light green linear leaves and sparse racemes composed of small, highly scented, bluish-white, bell-like flowers.
Flowering period   April–May.
Cultivation   Like other hyacinths, from which it has only relatively recently been separated, the plant needs a sunny position in light, sandy, well-drained soil. Plant bulbs September–October 6 in (15 cm) deep, and in dry weather water moderately until flowering.
Propagation   From seed or by bulbils, but it is really better to start with bulbs.
Care   After leaves turn yellow, dig up bulbs and keep them throughout summer in a dry, airy place. Plant in autumn. Protect the ground with straw or leaves during winter.
Other species   *B. dalmatica.*

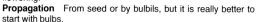

28 BLETILLA STRIATA
(Syn. *Bletia hyacinthina, Bletilla hyacinthina*)   U.S. zone 6

Family   Orchidaceae.
Origin   China, Japan.
Description   This small orchid, 12–16 in (30–40 cm) tall, furnished with numerous pseudobulbs, was introduced into Europe by the Spanish pharmacist Blet in 1802. It has lanceolate, plicate leaves and racemes composed of 5–10 flowers 1½–2-in (4–5 cm) across. These are purple-pink with a darker ruffled lip. There is also a variety with white flowers.
Flowering period   Summer.
Cultivation   Suitable for temperate climes, it grows well in semi-shade and in humus-rich, moist but well-drained soil. It can also be grown in pots or boxes, indoors or on the patio. Plant out in spring and water regularly, taking care to keep the soil always moist.
Propagation   By division of the root system in autumn or spring before plant growth resumes.
Care   The root system should be left in the ground during winter but has little resistance to frost. In milder climates it needs a good protective covering. Otherwise it can be buried in a bottomless box and covered with dead leaves or a pane of glass in winter. Potted plants also require shelter.

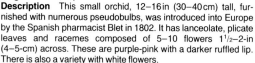

29 BULBOCODIUM VERNUM

U.S. zone 4

Family Liliaceae.
Origin Alps, mountains of southern Europe, Caucasus.
Description Corm with blackish tunic, three basal, linear or slightly lanceolate leaves, at first short and wrapping base of flowers, then, after flowers appear, longer, 4−6 in (10−15 cm). The 1−3 violet flowers, 4 in (10 cm) tall, have long-stalked lanceolate petals, joined only at base. The fruit is a capsule with three valves.
Flowering period February−April.
Cultivation A hardy species with beautiful early flowers, suitable for sunny borders but especially for rock gardens. Can also be grown in pots. Plant bulbs in autumn 3 in (8 cm) deep in any kind of soil provided it is well drained.
Propagation By growing on the cormels (cormlets) that form around the old corm.
Care Corms overwinter in ground without problem.

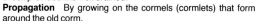

30 CALADIUM × HORTOLANUM

Angel's wings

U.S. zone 8

Family Araceae.
Origin Tropical regions of South America.
Description This group comprises numerous hybrids derived from *Caladium bicolor*. They are plants grown for their beautiful foliage. Up to 24−28 in (60−70 cm) tall, they have tuberous rhizomes and long-stalked leaves, shaped like a large arrow-head and sometimes wrinkled, ranging in color, according to variety, from dark green and yellowish-green, to red, crimson or white, often attractively veined or blotched.
Flowering period The pale pink flowers seldom appear and have no ornamental value.
Cultivation Caladiums are suitable for growing under glass, indoors, on the balcony and, in warm climates (not in Britain), even in the garden. They like half-shade and a growing medium made up of two parts garden soil, two parts peat, one part manure and one part sand, but a good peat-based compost will do. Plant the tuberous rhizomes in spring at 71°−77°F (22°−25°C), and when roots sprout, transplant into small pots. Feed with a liquid fertilizer every fortnight.
Propagation By division of rhizomes in winter.
Care Remove tuberous rhizomes in autumn, dry in an airy place for a week, clean, treat with a fungicide and keep in peat at 56°−61°F (13°−16°C).

31 CALOCHORTUS VENUSTUS
Mariposa lily   U.S. zone 6

Family Liliaceae.
Origin North America.
Description Bulbous plant with very long, thin, linear basal leaves, a stem of 24–28 in (60–70 cm) terminating in 1–2 white flowers, rarely yellow, red or violet, 3 in (7–8 cm) across, three-petaled, with a red spot in the center.
Flowering period Summer.

Cultivation Rather difficult to grow, calochortus is highly sensitive in winter to alternating periods of frost and thaw. It needs poor, dry, sandy, well-drained soil in full sun. After flowering, it requires a period of complete rest without water. Seldom successful outdoors in Britain, but it can be grown under glass, in pots. Keep it well sheltered when it flowers. Plant bulbs in autumn or spring 2 in (5 cm) deep and 10 in (25 cm) apart.
Propagation In midsummer, when growth is over, by separating the small bulbs that grow alongside the bigger ones.
Care Lift and store in dry peat or vermiculite, and replant in autumn.
Other species *C. albus*, *C. amabilis*, *C. barbatus*, *C. luteus*.

---

32 CAMASSIA LEICHTLINII
Zuamach, Quamash   U.S. zone 6

Family Liliaceae.
Origin North America.
Description Plant up to 48 in (120 cm) tall, with a whitish bulb, linear radical leaves 24 in (60 cm) long, and star-shaped flowers, creamy-white or light blue, 1 1/2 in (4 cm) across, in large terminal racemes that appear in spring before the leaves. 'Atrocaerulea' is blue to dark purple.
Flowering period Spring.

Cultivation This fairly hardy plant needs moist, heavy soil and a position in sun or partial shade. Averse to summer drought. Suitable for beds, borders, lake shores. Plant bulbs, possibly in clumps, in autumn 3–4 in (8–10 cm) deep and 6 in (15 cm) apart. Leave undisturbed for several years.
Propagation In September by division of bulbils that are produced rapidly and plentifully. Plants can also be easily obtained from seed but take 4–5 years to flower.
Care Bulbs overwinter in ground without problem.

33 CAMASSIA QUAMASH

(Syn. *C. esculenta*)   U.S. zone 6
Zuamach, Quamash

Family Liliaceae.
Origin North America.
Description Bulbous plant, 18–30 in (45–75 cm) tall, slender, linear radical leaves, often glaucous, about 20 in (50 cm) long, spike-like racemes of 10–40 starry flowers, blue or more rarely white, 1 in (3 cm) across. The bulbs are edible when cooked and for centuries have formed part of the diet of many Indian people.
Flowering period Late spring to early summer.
Cultivation Quite simple to grow, the plant needs moist, clay soil in semi-shade. Suitable for borders, small beds, large rock gardens – generally all positions with high humidity. Plant the bulbs in autumn 3–4 in (8–10 cm) deep, 6–10 in (15–25 cm) apart, and leave undisturbed for several years. Faded flowers should always be removed.
Propagation In September by division of the plentiful bulbils. Plants can also be obtained from seed, but take 4–5 years to flower.
Care Bulbs overwinter in ground without problem.

---

34 CANNA × HYBRIDA

U.S. zone 9

Family Cannaceae.
Origin Derived from American and tropical Asiatic species.
Description One of the most ancient plants used for ornamental purposes. Comprises numerous hybrids obtained from various tropical species. It has a short rhizome and, according to cultivar, a stem 24–64 in (60–160 cm) tall, large ovate or lanceolate leaves, green, red or brown, and inflorescences of 12–14 in (30–35 cm). These are composed of showy 4–6 in (10–15 cm) flowers, yellow, red or streaked.
Flowering period Summer.
Cultivation Plant rhizomes in March, 3 in (8 cm) deep, in pots, at temperature of 61°–65°F (16°–18°C), in compost made up of loam mixed with leaves, sand and manure. Water moderately at first, then gradually increase. In April–May plant out in a warm, sheltered position, in full sun and fertile soil, watering abundantly and regularly.
Propagation By division of rhizomes in early spring.
Care In mild climates cut down stems in autumn to a few centimeters and cover soil with straw or leaves. In colder climates lift rhizomes and keep them in peat at temperature not below 50°F (10°C).

35 CARDIOCRINUM GIGANTEUM

(Syn. *Lilium giganteum*)   U.S. zone 6
Giant Himalayan lily

Family Liliaceae.
Origin Himalayan region.
Description This majestic plant grows from an enormous bulb 7 in (17 cm) across and 8 in (20 cm) high, and may grow to a height of 10 ft (3 m). It has a strong stem, large dark green cordate leaves, and showy racemes of 20–25 funnel-shaped flowers, 6 in (15 cm) long, set horizontally along the scape. They are white with red-dish-brown streaks inside and fragrant.
Flowering period Summer.
Cultivation Dig a trench 20–24 in (50–60 cm) deep in a cool, shady position, and fill it with leafmold, manure, peat, sand and garden soil. Plant bulbs in autumn with tips just above the surface, 30 in (75 cm) apart. Bear in mind that they will die after they flower, leaving offsets to produce new flowers after 3–5 years. For continuous flowering, buy bulbs of different ages, water regularly in dry years.
Propagation From bulbils that appear following death of bulbs after flowering and that produce flowers after 3–5 years. Also from seed, in which case the first flowers will appear only after 7–8 years.
Care Mulch with leaves or straw during winter.
Other species *C. cordatum.*

---

36 CHIONODOXA LUCILIAE

Glory of the snow U.S. zone 5

Family Liliaceae.
Origin Asia Minor.
Description This small bulbous plant, not exceeding 8 in (20 cm) in height, has two linear basal leaves and a short stem terminating in a raceme of a few starry flowers, blue with a white center, formed of six petals joined together near the base in a short tube. Inside, the flattened filaments form a sort of cup. 'Alba' has white flowers and 'Rosea' and 'Pink Giant' have pink flowers.
Flowering period Early spring.
Cultivation Plant bulbs in autumn, 2 in (5 cm) deep and 4 in (10 cm) apart in any kind of soil, in sun or partial shade. Arranged in groups, they make a lovely early spring show. Ideal, too, for rock gardens. No feeding necessary. Leaves and flowers are attacked by slugs.
Propagation By dividing bulbils or from seed sown in June. Young plantlets can be planted out after a year.
Care The plant naturalizes easily and bulbs can remain in ground for years without problem.
Other species *C. gigantea, C. sardensis.*

37 CLIVIA MINIATA

(Syn. *Imantophyllum miniatum*)   **U.S. zone 10**
Kaffir lily

Family   Amaryllidaceae.
Origin   Southern Africa.
Description   The plant has thick, fleshy roots, strong stems of 16–18 in (40–45 cm), dark green, linear leaves coming from the base of the plant like a fan, and umbellate inflorescences, 8 in (20 cm) across, composed of 6–16 bell-like flowers generally scarlet with a yellow throat.
Flowering period   Spring or, if forced indoors, winter.
Cultivation   This delicate species can be grown outside only in very mild areas and in shady positions. It is not grown outdoors in the U.K. Ideal, however, for indoors or for greenhouse. Roots establish themselves within a few months in quite small pots, in a mixture consisting of one part potting loam, one part peat and one part sand. Water sporadically during winter, a period of partial rest, and abundantly during growth phase. Apply liquid fertilizer while growing. Repot every 3–4 years. Pots can be taken outside in warmer months.
Propagation   By division of clumps in autumn or after flowering, or from seed in spring in warm greenhouse or propagator.
Care   Roots outside die with first frosts and pots should be brought into greenhouse or indoors.
Other species   *C. nobilis.*

38 COLCHICUM AUTUMNALE

Naked boys, Autumn crocus, Meadow saffron   **U.S. zone 7**

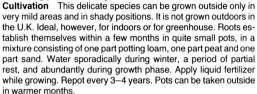

Family   Liliaceae.
Origin   Temperate Europe from France to Ukraine.
Description   In spring the corm produces four to five 8–10 in (20–25 cm) lanceolate, dark green leaves that are absent in autumn during flowering period. There are one or more flowers, in which the tube is uncolored and the lobes are lilac-pink. The anthers are yellow. 'Album' has white flowers; 'Roseum-plenum' double pink flowers. Corms, leaves and seeds are poisonous because they contain colchicine.
Flowering period   August–September.
Cultivation   The best known and most widespread species of colchicum. Plant corms in mid or late summer, during their rest period, 3 in (8 cm) deep, in a sunny or partially shaded position, in virtually any kind of well-drained soil. Make sure that in spring the abundant foliage does not suffocate smaller plantlets nearby. Suitable for rock gardens. Corms and leaves are eaten by slugs.
Propagation   Separating cormlets in summer, with flowers after 2 years, or from seed, with flowers after 4–5 years.
Care   Corms can be left undisturbed in ground for years.

39 COLCHICUM BYZANTINUM
Autumn crocus

U.S. zone 6

Family Liliaceae.
Origin Constantinople area.
Description Each corm, of considerable size and irregular in shape, may produce up to 20 flowers. The leaves 16 × 4 in (40 × 10 cm), appear in spring and are absent in late summer and early autumn, when the plant flowers. The crocus-shaped pale lilac-pink flowers, 4 in (10 cm) across, have characteristic styles 2 in (5 cm) long. Apparently the plant produces no seeds. The corms are poisonous.
Flowering period August–September.
Cultivation This is probably the most durable of colchicum species, and the corm can flower dry and unaided. Indoors, corms can simply be placed in a glass or other container without adding soil or applying water, and left alone – but if you want them to flower another year, plant them in the garden afterwards. In the garden, corms should be planted in midsummer, during the rest period, 3 in (8 cm) deep, in a sunny position or in partial shade, in any kind of well-drained soil. It is advisable to make sure that in spring the large leaves do not suffocate smaller developing plants nearby. Corms and leaves are attacked by slugs.
Propagation Separating cormlets in summer, with flowers after 2 years.
Care Corms can be left undisturbed in ground for years.

---

40 COLCHICUM SPECIOSUM

U.S. zone 6

Family Liliaceae.
Origin Asia Minor.
Description A species with very large, decorative flowers from which many interesting varieties have originated. In spring the corms produce four leaves 12 in (30 cm) long and 4 in (10 cm) wide, which last until June. The flowers, which appear in autumn, are violet on a white ground in the wild, but may be white, red or crimson in the numerous cultivated varieties. The segments of the reproductive organs, violet and concave to the tip, make the plants look something like tulips. The corms and seeds are poisonous because they contain colchicine.
Flowering period October.
Cultivation Plant corms in midsummer, during rest period, 4 in (10 cm) deep, in sun or partial shade, in well-drained soil. Ideal species for semi-naturalization but also suitable for growing in pots (the flowers are very durable) or for cut flowers. Make sure in spring that the large leaves do not suffocate smaller developing plants nearby. The corms and seeds are attacked by slugs.
Propagation By separating cormlets in summer, with flowers after 2 years, or from seed, with flowers after 7 years.
Care Corms can be left undisturbed in ground for years.

41 COLOCASIA ANTIQUORUM

(Syn. *Colocasia esculenta antiquorum*)   U.S. zone 8

Elephant's ear

Family Araceae.

Origin Tropical Asia.

Description This vigorous plant, up to 4 ft (1.2 m) tall, has roundish tuberous roots about 4 in (10 cm) across, bright green leaves shaped like arrow heads up to 24 in (60 cm) long and 18 in (45 cm) wide, persistent in warmer zones. Fairly small and insignificant yellow flowers. The tubers are edible.

Flowering period Summer.

Cultivation Grown for the beauty and exuberance of its foliage, this plant survives outside only in warmer months and is not grown outdoors in Britain. Pot tubers in greenhouse early spring and plant out in summer in moist soil with plenty of organic material, and in partial shade. It is wise to feed with a liquid fertilizer at least once a month.

Propagation In spring, by division of tubers, leaving at least one bud on each segment.

Care Remove tubers from ground in autumn, dry and keep in dry peat at 54°–61°F (12°–16°C) until spring. Permanent pot plants should be brought indoors.

---

42 CONVALLARIA MAJALIS

Lily of the valley   U.S. zone 4

Family Liliaceae.

Origin Cold and temperate zones of Europe, Asia and North America.

Description Plant 8–12 in (20–30 cm) tall with horizonal rhizome, upright, bicylindrical, double-edge stem, two bright green, elliptical-acute, paired leaves $2^1/_2 \times 6$ in (6 × 15 cm) that partly enfold the stem, laterally inclined racemes composed of 6–12 scented, campanulate, pendulous white flowers. The fruit is a red berry. 'Fortin's Giant' has large white flowers, 'Rosea' has pink flowers. The plant is poisonous.

Flowering period May–June.

Cultivation Typical plant of undergrowth, ideal as ground cover in cool and partly shaded position, in moist soil with plenty of humus. Plant rhizomes at the end of autumn just below surface. Can also be planted in pots and brought indoors for flowering during winter. Mulch with manure in autumn. The plant is subject to attack by gray mold.

Propagation By division of rhizomes in autumn or from seed under glass, in which case young plants take 2–3 years to flower.

Care Rhizomes survive well over winter in temperate or cold regions but may have problems in warmer zones.

43 CORYDALIS SOLIDA
(Syn. *C. bulbosa, Fumaria bulbosa*)　　　　　U.S. zone 6

Family　Papaveraceae.
Origin　Temperate Europe from France to Ukraine.
Description　Plant 6–8 in (15–20 cm) tall with upright glabrous stem, the lower stem leaf reduced to a scale, glaucous upper leaves deeply divided, somewhat resembling those of ferns. Tubular $^3/_4$-in (2-cm) flowers with pink corolla, violet throat, and slightly folded spur, grouped in upright raceme. Small yellow bulb.
Flowering period　April–May.
Cultivation　Does well in shade, in neglected corners, along walls or in rock garden, in poor, moist soil. Plant bulbs October 2–4 in (5–10 cm) deep. No watering or feeding necessary.
Propagation　Species multiplies naturally from seed but can also be propagated by bulb division when flowering is over.
Care　Bulbs can remain in ground without problem.
Other species　*C. cashmiriana, C. lutea.*

---

44 × CRINODONNA MEMORIA-CORSII
(Syn. *Amarcrinum*)　　　　　U.S. zone 9

Family　Amaryllidaceae.
Origin　Hybrid of horticultural origin.
Description　This intergeneric hybrid of *Amaryllis belladonna* and *Crinum moorei* has a bulb that produces two floral scapes 3 ft (1 m) in height. The second of these appears as the first is about to flower. The ligulate leaves are bright green, up to 24 in (60 cm) long, and there is a large terminal umbel of pink, trumpet-shaped flowers, 4 in (10 cm) across, which are highly scented and long-lasting.
Flowering period　Late summer–early autumn.
Cultivation　Although in mild regions it survives without problem in the garden, this species, which flowers best when the roots are tightly packed, is ideal for growing in pots. For best results, plant bulbs in February–March in greenhouse or indoors, individually in 6–8-in (15–20-cm) pots in a mixture of equal parts sand, peat and garden soil or any good potting compost. Feed and water regularly during growth period and gradually reduce as plant goes into winter rest. For flowers outdoors, plant bulbs in spring 4–6 in (10–15 cm) deep in the garden in a warm, sunny position.
Propagation　Divide small bulbs that develop alongside bigger ones.
Care　If planted outside, plants need mulch protection of leaves or straw in winter, or under pane of glass. Otherwise shelter pots at first sign of frost.

45 CRINUM BULBISPERMUM
(Syn. *C. longifolium*) **U.S. zone 9**

Family Amaryllidaceae.
Origin Southern Africa.
Description Stem 24–36 in (60–90 cm) tall; linear, glossy green persistent leaves up to 40 in (100 cm) long; umbels of about 20–24 funnel-shaped flowers 3–4 in (8–10 cm) long. These are fragrant and white, flushed pink outside. Bulb with papery tunic, like a tulip.
Flowering period Late summer.
Cultivation One of the hardier *Crinum* species but does not tolerate frost and should be grown outside only in milder climates, in warm, sunny, sheltered position, in fertile, moist, well-drained soil. Plant bulbs in spring 10–12 in (25–30 cm) deep. However, it is best to grow plants in small pots, since they flower better if roots are packed into a restricted space. Plant indoors or under glass in a mixture of equal parts peat, loam and sand. Alternatively, use any good proprietary potting compost. Water and feed regularly, and put outside only in warmer months. Suspend feeding in winter and reduce watering to minimum.
Propagation Grow on the small bulbs that develop alongside bigger ones.
Care If bulbs are in garden, protect them with a deep mulch of leaves or straw in winter and do not remove the plants' dead leaves until spring. Otherwise bring pots indoors at first sign of frost.

---

46 CRINUM × POWELLI
U.S. zone 9

Family Amaryllidaceae.
Origin Hybrid of horticultural origin.
Description Large bulb with a tunic, like a tulip, 8 in (20 cm) across, stem up to 18 in (45 cm) tall, very decorative glossy green, strap-like leaves, 20 in (50 cm) long, umbels of about 10 funnel-shaped flowers, 6 in (15 cm) long, light pink, white in 'Album.'
Flowering period Summer.
Cultivation A relatively hardy species that can be grown outdoors in mild climates if well protected from winter frost. Plant bulbs March–April 10–12 in (25–30 cm) deep, in warm, sunny position, perhaps sheltered by a wall, in fertile, well-drained soil. In colder climates it is best to grow them in quite small pots, indoors or in greenhouse, or outdoors when warmer, using a mixture of equal parts peat, loam and sand. Or use a good proprietary potting compost. Water and feed regularly during entire growing period.
Propagation In spring by removing and growing on the small bulbs that develop alongside bigger ones. Also from seed, but 5 years needed for flowering.
Care If grown in ground outdoors, do not transplant for several years and protect during winter with abundant mulch of leaves or straw. Otherwise shelter pots from frost.

Crinum × powelli 'Album.'

47 CROCOSMIA AUREA

(Syn. *Tritonia aurea*)
Copper tip, Falling stars

U.S. zone 9

Family Iridaceae.
Origin South Africa.
Description Plant with corm, 36 in (90 cm) tall, with light green, narrow, sword-like persistent leaves arranged fanwise around stem, and spikes of bright yellow flowers with prominent stamens.
Flowering period Summer.
Cultivation Relatively hardy plant with beautiful long-lasting flowers, ideal for borders or for cutting. Plant corms in spring 3 in (8 cm) deep, in fertile, well-drained soil, in warm, sunny position. Feed and water regularly throughout summer.
Propagation By division of corms during rest period or from seed in spring, with flowers after 2–3 years.
Care Remove corms from ground before cold weather, dry and keep in peat sheltered from frost until spring. In milder climates leave outside but protect well and remove dead leaves only in spring.

48 CROCOSMIA × CROCOSMIIFLORA

(Syn. *Montbretia crocosmiiflora, Tritonia crocosmiiflora*)
Montbretia

U.S. zone 7

Family Iridaceae.
Origin Hybrid of horticultural origin.
Description This group comprises different varieties obtained from hybridization of *Crocosmia aurea* and *Crocosmia pottsii*. They are very common plants, 24–32 in (60–80 cm) tall, with a corm, narrow sword-like persistent leaves arranged fanwise around stem, and spikes of yellow, orange or scarlet flowers, according to variety.
Flowering period Late summer.
Cultivation Fairly hardy plants, ideal for borders or for cutting. Cultivation as for *C. aurea*. Plant corms in spring, 3 in (8 cm) deep, in fertile, well-drained soil, in warm, sunny position. Feed and water regularly during summer.
Propagation By division of established clumps in rest period, or from seed in spring, with flowers after 2–3 years.
Care Remove corms from ground before cold weather, dry and keep in peat sheltered from frost until spring. In milder climates leave corms outside, well protected, and remove dead leaves only in spring.

Crocosmia × crocosmiiflora 'solfatare.'

49 CROCOSMIA MASONORUM

U.S. zone 8

Family Iridaceae.
Origin Southern Africa.
Description Regarded as the most beautiful of the *Crocosmia* species, this plant is 28–32 in (70–80 cm) tall and, like its relatives, grows from a corm. It has narrow, sword-shaped, fairly persistent leaves that are bigger than those of the other species, and spikes of large orange flowers, 1 in (2–3 cm) across, arranged in two rows and flowering successively along the spike.
Flowering period July–August.
Cultivation A fairly hardy plant, ideal for borders and for cut flowers. Grow like other *Crocosmia* species. Plant corms in spring, 3 in (8 cm) deep, in fertile, well-drained soil, in a warm, sunny position. Feed and water regularly during summer.
Propagation By division of established clumps in rest period, or from seed sown in spring.
Care Remove corms from ground before winter cold, dry and keep in peat, sheltered from frost, until spring. In milder climates corms may be left outside, well protected. Eliminate dead leaves only in spring.

---

50 CROCUS AUREUS

(Syn. *C. flavus, C. luteus*) U.S. zone 4
Dutch crocus

Family Iridaceae.
Origin Asia Minor. The species has originated many horticultural varieties.
Description Corm tunics with parallel fibers. Five to eight upright linear leaves, ¹/₄ in (2–4 mm) across, which after flowering may grow to a length of 20 in (50 cm). Simultaneously growing with leaves are the bright yellow flowers, with petals ³/₄–1¹/₄ in (1.5–3.5 cm) long, rounded at tip, with yellow stamens. The variety 'Dutch Yellow' is usually grown.
Flowering period February–March.
Cultivation Probably the oldest cultivated crocus, imported from Belgrade by the botanist Clusius in 1579, and still very widespread in flower beds and rock gardens. It forms splendid patches of yellow in February–March. It is an exceptionally hardy species, flourishing in any kind of well-drained soil. Plant corms in sun in autumn in small groups 3–4 in (8–10 cm) apart and 2–3 in (5–8 cm) deep. They tend to bury themselves of their own accord to a depth of 6–8 in (15–20 cm). Do not cut leaves after flowering and try to keep the ground dry during summer rest period.
Propagation In autumn, replant new corms that grow around the old one, or from seed in summer, with flowers after 3–4 years.
Care Corms can remain in ground and require no care.

51 CROCUS IMPERATI

Early crocus

Family Iridaceae.
Origin Southern Italy (Campania and Calabria).
Description Dark pear-shaped bulb; 3–5 linear $^1/_8$-in (1–1.2-mm) leaves, glossy dark green with a longitudinal white line. The stellate flowers, 4 in (10 cm) across, open completely; they have yellow throat and a perigonium violet inside and yellow, sometimes purple-veined, outside.
Flowering period January–March.
Cultivation Named after the sixteenth-century Italian botanist Ferrante Imperato, this especially early crocus (which flowers even in December in milder climates), strong and spreading easily, does well in sun in any kind of well-drained soil. Plant corms in autumn in small groups 3–4 in (8–10 cm) apart and 2–3 in (5–8 cm) deep. They tend to bury themselves to a depth of 6–8 in (15–20 cm).
Propagation In autumn replant new corms that grow around old one, or from seed in summer, with flowers after 3–4 years.
Care Corms remain in ground and require no care.

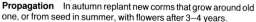

52 CROCUS SATIVUS

Saffron crocus

Family Iridaceae.
Origin Believed to be Asia Minor, but this is not certain.
Description Ciliate leaves, longer than flowers, present when latter bloom. Violet flowers open during the night and in bad weather; they have stigmas 1 in (2.5 cm) long that are scented, orange-red, sprouting from perigonium. The stigmas are cut and dried and used for making saffron.
Flowering period Autumn, September–October.
Cultivation The origin of *Crocus sativus*, cultivated for centuries in Europe to produce saffron, is lost in the mists of time, and today it is impossible to find it in its wild state. Many countries have stopped growing it because it is uneconomic. Plant corms in summer 3–4 in (8–10 cm) apart and 2–3 in (5–8 cm) deep, in warm, sheltered position and in well-drained soil.
Propagation A sterile plant that reproduces only by vegetative means. Divide established clumps.
Care Leave corms in ground all year round.

53 CROCUS TOMMASINIANUS

U.S. zone 4

Family Iridaceae.
Origin Dalmatia, Bosnia. There are many horiticultural varieties.
Description Two to four linear leaves, $^1/_4$ in (2–3 mm) wide, with a longitudinal silver line, well developed at time of flowering. Delicate stellate flowers that open completely have a lavender perigonium with white tube and silver-gray outer part. There are numerous horticultural varieties with pink, lilac, purple or white flowers.

Flowering period January–March.
Cultivation Named after the eighteenth-century Italian botanist Muzio de Tommasini, this crocus is one of the first to flower and naturalizes easily. Grows well in sun, in sheltered spot and in any kind of well-drained soil. Plant corms in autumn in small groups 3–4 in (8–10 cm) apart and 2–3 in (5–8 cm) deep. They tend to bury themselves to a greater depth.

Propagation In autumn from new corms that grow around old one, or from seed in summer, with flowers after 3–4 years.
Care Corms remain in ground and require no care.

---

54 CROCUS VERNUS

U.S. zone 4

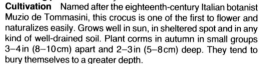

Family Iridaceae.
Origin Mountains of southern Europe, but not the Pyrenees. *Crocus vernus* has originated numerous garden varieties and hybrids with large flowers, known as Dutch crocuses.
Description The typical species has a rounded corm, 2–3 linear leaves $^1/_4$ in (3–4 mm) wide, with a white central vein, and generally one flower per corm, white or sometimes violet. Stamens with yellow anthers and white filaments. Style enlarged into three fanlike stigmas. Among the best-known varieties are 'Joan of Arc,' with large white flowers, and 'Purpureus Grandiflorus,' with large bright purple-blue flowers.

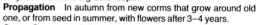

Flowering period February–April.
Cultivation Hardy species that grows well in any kind of soil, even moist, but cannot withstand long periods of drought. Naturalizes easily. Plant corms in autumn in small groups 3–4 in (8–10 cm) apart and 2–3 in (5–8 cm) deep. They tend to bury themselves further.

Propagation In autumn from new corms that grow around the old one, or from seed in summer, with flowers after 3–4 years.
Care Corms remain in ground and require no care.

Crocus vernus 'Negro Boy.'

55 CURTONUS PANICULATUS
(Syn. *Antholyza paniculata*)   U.S. zone 8

Family   Iridaceae.
Origin   Southern Africa.
Description   Plant with corm, 30–36 in (75–90 cm) tall, with upright stem and zigzag habit, linear-lanceolate, folded leaves, 3 in (8 cm) wide and 20–24 in (50–60 cm) long. The tubular orange-red flowers, 2 in (5 cm) long, are in loose spikes that are highly decorative.
Flowering period   Late summer.
Cultivation   Fairly hardy species, suitable for beds and borders, grows well in warm, sunny positions sheltered from winter frosts (if corms are to be left outside all year round), and in fertile, well-drained soil. Plant corms in autumn 6 in (15 cm) deep.
Propagation   In autumn by division of established clumps or from seed in greenhouse in spring.
Care   In mild climates leave corms in ground, well protected; in cold climates remove in autumn, dry and keep frost-free until spring.

---

56 CYCLAMEN COUM
(Syn. *C. ibiricum, C. orbiculatum, C. vernum*)   U.S. zone 6

Family   Primulaceae.
Origin   Southeastern Europe, Asia Minor.
Description   Tuberous plant, 3 in (7–8 cm) tall, with ovate-cordate leaves, dark red on lower side and silver spotted on upper side. Flowers with broad lobes, pink, crimson or white with purple spots.
Flowering period   From winter to early spring.
Cultivation   Hardy cyclamen grows well in undergrowth and therefore in a shady position, in light, permeable soil rich in organic material. It is also suitable for rock gardens. Plant tubers midsummer 4–6 in (10–15 cm) apart and 2 in (5 cm) deep. Apply leafmold as a fertilizer in early spring. The species is attacked by many pests and diseases (thrips, mites, cutworms, nematodes, molds, slugs and snails, etc.).
Propagation   Never divide tubers, even if they grow steadily in size and survive for many years. Cyclamens, in fact, propagate themselves, often spontaneously, only through seeds. Planted in autumn, these will germinate the following spring.
Care   The tubers are highly sensitive to transplanting and should be left undisturbed.

57 CYCLAMEN HEDERIFOLIUM
(Syn. *Cyclamen Neapolitanum*)

U.S. zone 5

Family Primulaceae.
Origin Southern coasts of Europe from Spain to Greece.
Description Tuber globose or depressed-globose, long-lived, often becoming very large. Leaves with small, often twisted, pink stalk and pubescent blade, usually ivy-shaped but variable, green with silvery-green on upper surface and purple beneath, present in winter. Single, usually odorless flower, with $1/4–1/2$-in (6–12-mm) peduncle and corolla with pink tube and pale pink, purple-streaked fringes. Pure white flowers are rare in the wild but common in cultivation.
Flowering period August–October.

Cultivation Usually found wild in scrub or deciduous woodland. Hardy and adaptable for gardens. Grows well in either sun or partially shaded sites, preferring a light, well-drained, humus-rich soil. Suitable also for the rock garden. Plant tubers midsummer, 4–6 in (10–15 cm) apart and 2 in (5 cm) deep. Apply light mulch in late autumn or early spring but avoid smothering the foliage. The species is attacked by numerous animal and plant parasites (see previous entry).

Propagation The tubers cannot readily be divided and this must never be attempted. Will self-sow freely when growing well. Harvested seed should always be sown fresh, and will germinate within 2–4 months.
Care Tubers can be transplanted at almost any time if the soil is workable and not too cold. However, the best time to plant is late July–early August, just as the roots are becoming active again after their summer rest. Tubers should be left undisturbed in the ground.

58 CYCLAMEN PERSICUM
Florist's cyclamen

tender

Family Primulaceae.
Origin From the Aegean to Iran.
Description This species has originated numerous large-flowered varieties, many of which are grown as winter house plants. Tuber rounded and flattened at either end, leaves almost always beautifully variegated, single pedunculate flowers with large corollas of $1 1/4–1 1/2$ in (3–4 cm), pink, red, lavender or white, according to variety.
Flowering period Winter or spring, indoors.

Cultivation Often grown on commercial scale, the many varieties derived from this species of cyclamen are not generally hardy and are susceptible to excessive heat or standing water. To get cyclamens to flower indoors in winter, sow August–September in a mixture of equal parts leafmold, sand and peat. Place pots in darkness at temperature of 65°–68°F (18°–20°C); after 5–6 weeks the plantlets appear. When they have two leaves transplant them into small pots and keep sheltered until spring, watering and feeding regularly. Transplant them a second time, taking care that they are not in direct sunlight. First flowers will appear in October.

Propagation Generally from seed August–September.
Care During the rest period, tip the pots sideways so that the tubers dry out properly.

Left: *Cyclamen persicum* 'Cattleya.'
Right: *Cyclamen persicum* 'Triumph White.'

59 DAHLIA × CULTORUM
Dahlia   **tender**

Family Compositae.
Origin Horticultural hybrids derived from species originating in Mexico (*D. coccinea, D. pinnata*, etc.).
Description The description *Dahlia × cultorum* groups together a very large number of hybrids of complex origin, principally obtained from several Mexican species. Dahlias have thick tuberous roots, strong, upright, fleshy stems; opposite, pinnate leaves; and flowers that vary in form, size and color. They come in all colors, with the exception of blue. As in all the Compositae, the flower heads, incorrectly called flowers, are actually inflorescences made up of two principal types of flower: small tubular flowers that form the central disk, and ligulate flowers, arranged along the outer circumference of the disk, which constitute the individual ray-florets.

Dahlias are normally classified in groups based on the form and dimensions of the flower heads. Broadly speaking, there is a distinction between bedding dahlias, including dwarf varieties, and border dahlias.

BORDER DAHLIAS
On the basis of flower form, these dahlias are divided into the following principal groups:

Single-flowered: Plants 16–28 in (40–70 cm) tall, flower heads 4 in (10 cm) or less across, with a loose central disk and a single ring of red, lilac, pink or scarlet ligulate flowers. Varieties include 'Nellie Geerlings,' scarlet, and 'Princess Marie José,' lilac-pink.

Anemone-flowered: Plants up to 3 ft (1 m) tall, flower heads 4 in (10 cm) across, with a compact central disk made up of numerous tubular flowers and with one or more rings of flat ligulate flowers. Varieties include 'Comet,' chestnut-brown, and 'Lucy,' white with yellow disk.

Collarette: Plants up to 4 ft (1.2 m) tall, flower heads 4 in (10 cm) across, with a central disk, an outer ring of large, flat ligulate flowers, and an inner ring with a shorter ligule (collar). The two types of ligulate flowers may be of contrasting colors. Varieties include 'Can-Can,' pink ray and yellow collar.

Peony-flowered: Plants 3 ft (1 m) tall, flower heads 4 in (10 cm) across, with a central disk and two or more rings of flat ligulate flowers, orange, red or purple.

Decorative: Plants 3–5 ft (1–1.5 m), completely double flower heads, without central disk but with many ligulate flowers, usually large and flat with a blunt margin. There is a vast range of colors, very popular for the production of cut flowers. This group is in turn subdivided into five sections according to the dimensions of the flower heads: Giant (more than 10 in/25 cm across) (e.g. 'Hamari Girl,' pink); Large (8–10 in/20–25 cm) (e.g. 'Robert Damp,' yellow); Medium (6–8 in/15–20 cm) (e.g. 'Sterling Silver,' white); Small (4–6 in/10–15 cm) (e.g. 'Snow Queen,' white); and Miniature (under 4 in/10 cm) (e.g. 'Doris Duke,' pink).

Ball: Plants 4 ft (1.2 m) tall with spherical, completely double flower heads, like a pompon, without central disk, composed of numerous ligulate flowers, spirally arranged, the ligule having a rounded, blunt tip and being curved inward for at least half of its length. The group is subdivided into two sections: Ball (4–6 in/10–15 cm) (e.g. 'Esmonde,' yellow) and Miniature (2–4 in/5–10 cm) (e.g. 'Florence Vernon,' lilac).

Pompon: Plants 4 ft (1.2 m) tall, similar to ball varieties but with flower heads maximum 2 in (5 cm) across, and ligulate flowers

curving inward along the entire length. Varieties include 'Little Conn,' dark red, and 'Pom of Poms,' scarlet.

Cactus: Plants 3–5 ft (1–1.5 m) tall, with flower heads of varying size, completely double, without central disk, composed of numerous ligulate flowers, not very compact, with narrow, furled ligules. The group is subdivided into five sections, according to the dimensions of the flower heads (sizes similar to those given for decoratives): Giant, Large, Medium, Small and Miniature. 'Danny' is a pink giant, 'Charmer' a purple miniature.

Semi-cactus: Plants 3–5 ft (1–1.5 m) tall, similar to preceding group, but with fuller flower heads and larger, flatter ligules for at least half their length. The group is subdivided into five sections, according to the dimensions of the flower heads: Giant, Large, Medium, Small and Miniature. Varieties include 'Respectable,' yellow giant, and 'Lynne Bartholomew,' purple-red miniature.

BEDDING DAHLIAS

These plants are 12–20 in (30–50 cm) tall, with flower heads 2–3 in (5–7 cm) across, single, semi-double or double, white or in various shades of yellow, pink, red or lilac. Varieties include 'Fascination,' pink or purple.

Flowering period Midsummer to late autumn.

Cultivation Dahlias are rather delicate plants that do not survive in the ground over the winter and do best in temperate climates and positions in full sun. Plant tuberous roots in mid spring 4–6 in (10–15 cm) deep and 24–36 in (60–90 cm) apart in deeply dug, fertile, moist but well-drained soil, well manured. When planting, fix stakes in ground, for later attachment of stems. In order to grow well, dahlias need plentiful and regular watering, preferably around the base of the plants rather than applied from top. In drier climates mulching is advisable. For continuous flowering, it is best to remove dead flowers regularly. This prevents the formation of seeds, a process that exhausts the plant unnecessarily and makes the development of secondary flowers more difficult. Dahlias are subject to attack by many harmful pests, including moths, aphids, red spider, nematodes and, among plant parasites, soft root rot, which causes blackening and rotting of tuberous roots with the appearance of small black specks, gray mold and various viruses that cause mottled or curled leaves or stunted plants.

Propagation In spring by division of tuberous roots. This rather delicate operation should be carried out with a sharp knife, making sure that each part is connected to a portion of stem, at the base of which the shoots will develop.

With a little experience and patience, the plants can also be propagated from cuttings, the method adopted by professional growers and enthusiasts. Plant the tubers under glass at the end of winter at a fairly high temperature, 61°–65°F (16°–18°C), leaving the collar at soil level. Water abundantly to encourage growth. When the shoots reach 2–3 in (5–8 cm), remove them, retaining the area around the collar, and pot in a mixture of sand and garden soil. Atmospheric humidity should be very high so as to prevent cuttings from drying out. After 10–15 days the shoots will have developed a sufficient root system and can be potted up. In late spring, when the danger of frost has receded, the young plants should be planted out. The dwarf varieties may also be propagated from seed sown under glass in spring. They will flower from midsummer.

Care In late autumn, as soon as the leaves begin to turn black from frost, cut down stems to about 4 in (10 cm) above ground level, and gently dig up the tuberous roots, taking care not to damage the collar. Throw out any damaged tubers; clean off the soil

from sound ones and let dry upside-down for a week (so as to eliminate water from hollow stems). Then store in peat in a dry place and at a temperature of 41°–46°F (5°–8°C) throughout winter.

60   DIERAMA PULCHERRIMUM
Wand flower

Family   Iridaceae.
Origin   South Africa.
Description   A very elegant cormous plant with linear-lanceolate leaves 2–3 ft (60–90 cm) long and slender stems about 3 ft (1 m) in height that curve inward near the tip where they bear beautiful arching sprays of funnel-shaped, pendulous flowers, ³/₄ in (2 cm) long, generally reddish-purple. Varieties include 'Album,' with white flowers, 'Heron,' wine-red, and 'Skylark,' violet.
Flowering period   From late summer to autumn.
Cultivation   This rather delicate member of the Iridaceae cannot stand cold climates and needs a sheltered position in full sun and in well-drained soil. Plant corms in spring or autumn 4–6 in (10–15 cm) deep and 12–20 in (30–50 cm) apart. Leave undisturbed for several years since they react badly to transplanting. Take care the plant does not suffer from drought.
Propagation   By division of established clumps; lift the corms in autumn and keep until spring or plant under glass for flowering after 12–16 months. The plant can also be propagated from seed in the greenhouse, in spring, with flowers after 3 years.
Care   Corms may be left outside in winter, with adequate protection, in warmest zones.

61 DIOSCOREA BATATAS
Chinese yam

Family Dioscoreaceae.
Origin China, Sunda Islands.
Description Large tubers up to 28–32 in (70–80 cm) long, which tend to probe deep into the ground; twining stems, up to 23–33 ft (7–10 m) long, with many beautiful ovate, glossy leaves, at the axils of which tiny bulbils may develop; small, insignificant, greenish-white flowers in racemes at leaf axils, pleasantly cinnamon-scented.
Flowering period Summer.
Cultivation Cultivated in China for many centuries, this plant possesses a very large edible tuber which, when cooked, has an agreeable taste similar to that of a potato. Introduced into France in the nineteenth century, it grows well in temperate zones and is a useful rambler for pergolas and trellises. Plant in spring, in a warm, sunny position and in deep, fertile soil. Watering should be plentiful in growing period.
Propagation From stem cutting several centimeters long to root under glass during summer.
Care In unsheltered positions and colder climates it is advisable to protect roots in winter with a thick covering of dry leaves.

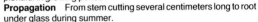

62 DRACUNCULUS VULGARIS
Dragon arum

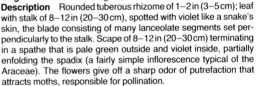

Family Araceae.
Origin Mediterranean region, from Gibraltar to Black Sea.
Description Rounded tuberous rhizome of 1–2 in (3–5 cm); leaf with stalk of 8–12 in (20–30 cm), spotted with violet like a snake's skin, the blade consisting of many lanceolate segments set perpendicularly to the stalk. Scape of 8–12 in (20–30 cm) terminating in a spathe that is pale green outside and violet inside, partially enfolding the spadix (a fairly simple inflorescence typical of the Araceae). The flowers give off a sharp odor of putrefaction that attracts moths, responsible for pollination.
Flowering period May–June.
Cultivation It is not difficult to grow this hardy species. Plant out rhizomes in autumn in a warm, shaded spot in humus-rich, moist but well-drained soil. Water abundantly during summer.
Propagation By division of rhizomes during rest period or from seed in greenhouse.
Care During winter the rhizomes can be left outside, protected with a mulch of dry leaves.

63 ENDYMION HISPANICUS

(Syn. *Scilla hispanica, S. campanulata, Hyacinthoides hispanica*) U.S. zone 5

Spanish bluebell, Spanish hyacinth

Family Liliaceae.
Origin Western Mediterranean.
Description Plant 8–20 in (20–50 cm) tall with rounded bulb, furrowed, linear leaves, and a strong scape terminating in a raceme of 5–15 bell-like, pendulous flowers, $^1/_2$–$^3/_4$ in (1–2 cm) long, violet, almost unscented, with tips of petals curving outward.
Flowering period March–June.
Cultivation This species, cultivated since the early 1600s, is particularly suitable for positions of light shade, as in open undergrowth, or in rock gardens. Plant bulbs end of winter 4–6 in (10–15 cm) deep in moist but not swampy ground, rich in organic substances. Bulbs should not be transplanted as they have no tunic and are thus rather fragile.
Propagation In autumn by separating bulblets that form around bulbs, or from seed, on leafmold, in which case flowers appear only after 5–6 years. The species tends to naturalize and spread freely.
Care Bulbs can be left outside during winter.
Other species *E. italicus, E. non-scriptus, Scilla non-scripta.*

---

64 ERANTHIS CILICICA

U.S. zone 5

Family Ranunculaceae.
Origin Asia Minor, Cilicia.
Description Very similar to *Eranthis hyemalis*, it differs from the latter in having larger and slightly bronze leaves, a pink scape and somewhat bigger flowers.
Flowering period Winter.
Cultivation Perhaps even hardier than *E. hyemalis*, it flowers later. In the wild it grows on rocky substrata. It is therefore especially suitable for rock gardens in full sun. Plant rhizomes in autumn 1 in (2–3 cm) deep. The plant dies down completely in summer.
Propagation Remove rhizomes from ground after leaves fade, divide and replant immediately.
Care Rhizomes may be left outside throughout the year in almost any climate without protection.

65   ERANTHIS HYEMALIS
Winter aconite   U.S. zone 6

Family   Ranunculaceae.
Origin   Central and southern Europe.
Description   Rhizome with small, irregular tubercles, upright, glabrous stem, radical leaves with stalk of 2–4 in (5–10 cm), peltate, with pinnate blade. Flowers single, 1 in (2–3 cm) across, composed of 6–8 yellow petal segments.
Flowering period   February–March.
Cultivation   These delightful winter flowers have no special climatic requirements and adapt to all types of soil provided it is not too dry. Plant rhizomes in autumn 1 in (2–3 cm) deep, after soaking for 24 hours. They should be in a sunny position during winter and if possible in partial shade during summer (as, for example, beneath large broadleaved trees). Leaves develop after winter flowers, forming attractive carpets of greenery in spring, but they quickly dry out as it gets warmer.
Propagation   Once established, the plant spreads naturally from seed, forming lovely compact colonies. The species can also be propagated by division of rhizomes after leaves have faded.
Care   Rhizomes can be left outside throughout the year in most climates without protection.

66   EREMURUS ROBUSTUS
Foxtail lily   U.S. zone 6

Family   Liliaceae.
Origin   Turkestan.
Description   Highly spectacular plant, up to 10 ft (3 m) tall, with large fleshy roots, arranged star-like, linear basal leaves up to 3 ft (1 m) long, a round, stiff, fleshy flower scape, terminating in a characteristically pointed raceme composed of stellate flowers in various colors ranging from pink to ocher-yellow. Since the leaves disappear when the flowers fade, it is best to locate the plants at the back of the border.
Flowering period   June and July.
Cultivation   Success in growing this plant, which is not particularly difficult, depends to a large extent on careful preparation of the soil, which must be fertile, manured, sandy and very well drained (the plant is highly susceptible to root rot). Plant roots in September, in full sun, a few centimeters deep and 28–40 in (70–100 cm) apart.
Propagation   Roots should be left undisturbed for at least 5 years before dividing them, in autumn.
Care   During winter protect soil with straw or dry leaves.
Other species   E. bungei, E. olgae, E. himalaicus. There are also garden hybrids.

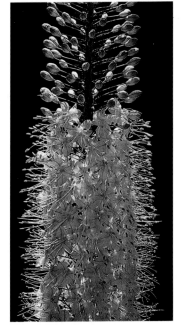

67 ERYTHRONIUM AMERICANUM

Common fawn-lily, Trout lily   U.S. zone 3

Family Liliaceae.
Origin Eastern regions of North America, from Canada to Florida.
Description This small cormous species has linear-lanceolate leaves typically streaked with brown; an upright scape, furled at the tip; and single nodding, stellate flowers 2 in (5 cm) across, consisting of six reflexing yellow petals, brown-streaked at base. They open only in the warmth of the sun.
Flowering period March–June.
Cultivation This hardy species, of delicate appearance, grows well in semi-shade in sandy, fertile soil that is regularly manured. Plant corms in autumn 6 in (15 cm) deep and 4–6 in (10–15 cm) apart. Take care they do not become dry while being planted out. They cannot withstand excessively hot, dry summers, and they dislike being transplanted.
Propagation From cormlets in late summer, removing them from ground and replanting them immediately so as to avoid drying out. The plant can also be propagated from seed, flowering after 5 years.
Care Corms can be left undisturbed in ground for several years and require no special care.

68 ERYTHRONIUM DENS-CANIS

Dog-tooth violet, European fawn-lily   U.S. zone 3

Family Liliaceae.
Origin Warm zones of Europe and dry belt of southern Siberia.
Description White spindle-shaped corm; upright, glabrous, reddish scape, curved at tip; lanceolate leaves, glaucous with purple and white spots, especially on upper surface. Single flower, composed of six, backward-curving pink petals, prominent violet anther about $1/4$ in (7–8 mm) long, white style. There are many cultivated varieties with violet, pink, red and white flowers.
Flowering period March–April.
Cultivation Widely found growing wild in broadleaved woods both in lowland and upland areas, this hardy species, of delicate appearance, should be planted in autumn in semi-shade and fertile, manured soil. Take care that corms do not become dry while being planted out. Plant 6 in (15 cm) deep and 4–6 in (10–15 cm) apart. They cannot withstand excessively dry, hot summers, and they dislike being transplanted.
Propagation From cormlets in late summer, removing them from ground and replanting them immediately. The plant can also be propagated from seed, flowering after 5 years.
Care Corms can be left undisturbed in ground for several years without special care.

69 ERYTHRONIUM REVOLUTUM
Mahogany fawn-lily

Family Liliaceae.
Origin California.
Description Plant about 12 in (30 cm) tall, this plant is one of the most beautiful of the genus. It has lanceolate leaves, streaked with brown, an upright scape, curved at the tip and terminating in a single pendulous flower composed of six lanceolate petals, white, pink or purple, according to variety. The stamens are typically swollen.
Flowering period May.
Cultivation Plant corms of this hardy species in autumn in semi-shade and in fertile, manured soil. Take care that corms do not become dry while being planted out. Plant 6 in (15 cm) deep and 4–6 in (10–15 cm) apart. They cannot withstand excessively dry, hot summers, and they dislike being transplanted.
Propagation From cormlets in late summer, removing them from ground and replanting them immediately so as to avoid drying out. The plant can also be propagated from seed, flowering after 5 years.
Care Bulbs can be left undisturbed for several years without special care.

---

70 ERYTHRONIUM TUOLUMNENSE

Family Liliaceae.
Origin California.
Description Vigorous plant, about 12 in (30 cm) tall, with two broad lanceolate leaves, yellowish-green without markings, upright scape terminating in small stellate 1½-in 4-cm flowers composed of six golden-yellow petals.
Flowering period Spring.
Cultivation Plant corms of this hardy species in autumn in semi-shade and in fertile, manured, moist but well-drained soil. Take care that corms do not become dry while being planted out. Plant 6 in (15 cm) deep and 4–6 in (10–15 cm) apart. They cannot withstand excessively dry, hot summers, and they dislike being transplanted.
Propagation When the plants become too dense, remove corms from ground at the end of summer, separate cormlets and replant them immediately, taking care that they do not dry out. The plant can also be propagated from seed, flowering after 5 years.
Care Corms can be left undisturbed for several years without special care.

71 EUCHARIS GRANDIFLORA

(Syn. *Eucharis amazonica*) **tender**
Amazon lily

Family Amaryllidaceae.
Origin South America, Colombia.
Description Elongated bulb, with tunic, bright green ovate leaves 8–12 in (20–30 cm) long, scape of 12–24 in (30–60 cm) terminating in umbel of 3–6 white flowers, 3 in (7–8 cm) across. These are delicately scented and similar to some kinds of narcissus.
Flowering period Winter, but may be forced into flower at any time of year.
Cultivation Extremely sensitive to frost, this species must be grown in a pot, in the greenhouse or indoors, in a well-lit position but sheltered from direct sun and at a high temperature throughout the year. Plant bulbs in early spring in a mixture of equal parts peat, leafmold and sand, with the addition of bonemeal and manure, or use a good proprietary potting compost. The flowers will appear soon afterward. Water abundantly and feed every fortnight until autumn, then reduce water and suspend feeding to allow plant a short rest period. Repot every 2–3 years.
Propagation By separating bulblets, preferably July–August.
Care The bulbs react favorably to transplanting every 2–3 years, but care should be taken not to damage roots.

---

72 EUCOMIS BICOLOR

Pineapple lily **U.S. zone 10**

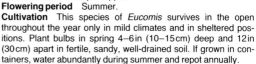

Family Liliaceae.
Origin South Africa.
Description Impressive bulbous plant with big bright green leaves, loose, wavy at edges, arranged in basal rosette. Sturdy scape, 14–16 in (35–40 cm), terminating in dense raceme of stellate flowers, 1 in (2.5 cm) across, green with lilac border. The inflorescence is surmounted by a characteristic rosette of leaf bracts similar to those of the pineapple.
Flowering period Summer.
Cultivation This species of *Eucomis* survives in the open throughout the year only in mild climates and in sheltered positions. Plant bulbs in spring 4–6 in (10–15 cm) deep and 12 in (30 cm) apart in fertile, sandy, well-drained soil. If grown in containers, water abundantly during summer and repot annually.
Propagation By separating bulblets in spring, with flowers after 2–3 years, or from seed, with flowers after 5–6 years.
Care Protect the ground during winter with a generous mulch of straw or leaves, or shelter pot-grown plants.

73 EUCOMIS PUNCTATA

(Syn. *E. comosa*) U.S. zone 10
Pineapple lily

Family Liliaceae.
Origin South Africa.
Description Rough, conical bulb, smooth leaves, up to 20 in (50 cm) long, lower side spotted reddish-brown; scape 12–16 in (30–40 cm) tall, terminating in an inflorescence made up of numerous scented flowers, greenish-white with lilac throat.
Flowering period Summer to autumn.
Cultivation This species of *Eucomis* also survives in open throughout the year only in mild climates and sheltered positions. Plant bulbs in spring 4–6 in (10–15 cm) deep and 12 in (30 cm) apart in fertile, sandy, well-drained soil. If grown in containers, water abundantly during summer and renew soil frequently.
Propagation By separating bulblets in spring, with flowers after 2–3 years, or from seed, with flowers after 5–6 years.
Care Protect soil during winter with mulch of straw or leaves, or shelter pot-grown plants.

74 FREESIA × HYBRIDA

Freesia U.S. zone 9

Family Iridaceae.
Origin Hybrids of horticultural origin obtained from South African parents.
Description Plant with corm, slender stems, 12–18 in (30–45 cm) tall, curved at tip, linear-lanceolate leaves, spikes of upright, one-sided, trumpet-shaped, fragrant flowers in colors ranging from white or yellow to lilac, orange, red, and blue.
Flowering period Spring, when grown in open.
Cultivation In temperate regions freesias may be grown outside (but select varieties suitable for this), in a warm, sheltered position; but U.S. zone 10 may be too warm. Plant corms end summer in light, fertile soil 2 in (5 cm) deep and 2–4 in (5–10 cm) apart, to flower following spring. In cold climates it is best to plant corms in spring in pots in a mixture of soil, sand and peat (or a good proprietary potting compost). Shelter plants indoors or in greenhouse during winter. In both cases, water plentifully and feed once a month throughout growing period.
Propagation By separating the small corms that form around larger ones, end summer. It is also easy to propagate plants from seed.
Care Shelter pots over winter in cold house or in a warm corner indoors. In U.S. zone 9, where corms can remain in ground, they need suitable protection.

75 FRITILLARIA IMPERIALIS
Crown imperial

Family Liliaceae.
Origin Western Asia.
Description Large scaly bulb; upright, sturdy stem, 2½−4¾ in (6−12 cm) tall, which for half its length bears numerous sessile, linear-lanceolate, glossy leaves; a crown of 4−7 big, nodding bells surmounted by "crown" of leaves. The flowers have yellow-brown, scarlet-veined petals and projecting styles. Varieties include 'Aurora,' orange-yellow flowers, 'Lutea,' yellow, and 'Rubra,' red. The plant is poisonous.
Flowering period April−May.
Cultivation This splendid plant, introduced to the imperial park in Vienna in 1576, is relatively easy to grow. It needs a temperate climate, a semi-shaded position and fertile, very well-drained soil. Plant bulbs, which must be carefully handled and not allowed to become dry, in August 8 in (20 cm) deep, and set at a slight angle so that water does not get into them. Place a handful of sand below the bulbs. Mulch every year with manure, and water regularly.
Propagation In summer by separating small bulbs which form around larger ones (this must be done with great care and does not always produce results), or from seed, with flowers after 5−6 years.
Care Bulbs like to be left undisturbed in ground. In cold climates give a winter mulch of straw or leaves.

---

76 FRITILLARIA MELEAGRIS
Snake's-head fritillary

Family Liliaceae.
Origin Central Europe.
Description Pear-shaped bulb; upright cylindrical stem, up to 18 in (45 cm) tall; 4−6 linear leaves with central channel; pendulous, campanulate flowers with petals colored in a checkered pattern of pale violet and dark purple. There are also selected varieties in brown, yellow, white, etc. Varieties include 'Alba,' with white, green-veined flowers, 'Poseidon,' purple, and 'Saturnus,' violet-red.
Flowering period April.
Cultivation A flower of wet fields and meadows, this fritillary needs cool, fertile soil, treated with a little peat or sand, in a shaded position. It withstands winter temperatures. Plant bulbs at an angle in autumn, 6 in (15 cm) deep, and water regularly.
Propagation In summer by separating small bulbs which form alongside bigger ones, or from seed, with flowers after 5−6 years.
Care The bulbs are delicate and must be handled carefully. Leave in ground over winter.

77 FRITILLARIA PERSICA

Family Liliaceae.
Origin Western Asia.
Description Bulb formed of two scales; stiff upright stem, 20–24 in (50–60 cm) tall, with numerous pale green linear-subulate leaves, terminating in a pyramidal raceme of 10–50 pendulous, campanulate purple flowers, $^3/_8$–$^3/_4$ in (10–20 mm) long. The variety 'Adiyaman,' up to 4 ft (1.2 m) tall, is particularly lovely.
Flowering period March–April.
Cultivation With *Fritillaria imperialis* this was one of the first fritillaries imported from the Far East, and it has therefore been cultivated for several centuries. It needs fertile soil and a warm, sunny position, perhaps in the shelter of a south-facing wall. Plant bulbs at an angle, in August, 6 in (15 cm) deep, and water regularly.
Propagation In summer by separating small bulbs which form alongside the bigger ones, or from seed, with flowers after 5–6 years.
Care The bulbs are very delicate and must be handled carefully. In cold climates during winter it is advisable to protect ground with leaves or straw.

78 GALANTHUS NIVALIS
Snowdrop U.S. zone 6

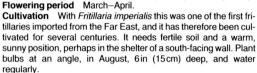

Family Amaryllidaceae.
Origin Europe and Caucasus.
Description Ovoid bulb with dark tunic; upright stem, 6–10 in (15–25 cm) tall; leaves strap-shaped, rounded at tip; single pendulous flower with outer petals larger and white, inner petals smaller and spotted green. Varieties include 'Flore-plena,' with double flowers, and 'Viridapicis,' with green spots also on outer petals.
Flowering period February–March.
Cultivation Snowdrops grow wild in many parts of Europe in cool, wet woodlands. The numerous garden varieties, hardy and easily grown, need fertile, moist but well-drained soil, and a partially shaded position. Plant bulbs September 2–4 in (5–10 cm) deep and 4–6 in (10–15 cm) apart. They are subject to attack by nematodes.
Propagation By separating bulblets immediately after flowering and replanting them immediately so that roots do not have time to dry. Snowdrops naturalize freely.
Care Bulbs can be left undisturbed in ground for several years and need no winter protection.

79 GALTONIA CANDICANS
Summer hyacinth

Family   Liliaceae.
Origin   Africa.
Description   Plant up to 3 ft (1 m) tall, with a large rounded bulb, linear-lanceolate basal leaves, glaucous green and 30 in (75 cm) long, a stiff upright stem, rounded in section, terminating in an inflorescence of 20–30 pendulous, campanulate flowers, 1½ in (4 cm) long, white with green tints, delicately scented.
Flowering period   End summer.
Cultivation   This fairly hardy plant needs fertile, well-drained soil and a sunny position. Plant bulbs in April 6 in (15 cm) deep. In colder regions they are best planted in pots under glass in autumn, thus getting early flowers.
Propagation   By separating small bulbs that form alongside bigger ones, or from seed under glass in spring.
Care   In mild climates the bulbs can be left in ground over winter provided it is not wet and is protected with a generous layer of dead leaves. In colder climates it is better to dig up bulbs and keep them in a dry place.

80 GERANIUM TUBEROSUM
Tuberous geranium

Family   Geraniaceae.
Origin   Warm regions of Europe and dry belt of southern Siberia.
Description   This species of *Geranium* has thick roots that form 1–3 ovoid tubercles. The stem is upright, the leaves are all basal with the blade divided into 5–7 pinnate segments, and the flowers, ⁵/₁₆–½ in (8–12 mm) across, have violet-purple petals with darker veining.
Flowering period   March–May.
Cultivation   Often found wild in fields and grasslands, this species is easy to grow, requiring a dry, sunny position and well-drained soil. Plant the large tuberous roots in spring 2 in (5 cm) deep and 10–12 in (25–30 cm) apart.
Propagation   By dividing roots in early spring, from seed or from young shoot cuttings under glass.
Care   Roots can stay outside all year round and need no special care.

81 GLADIOLUS (hybrids)
Sword lily

tender

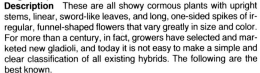

Family Iridaceae.

Origin Hybrids of complex derivation.

Description These are all showy cormous plants with upright stems, linear, sword-like leaves, and long, one-sided spikes of irregular, funnel-shaped flowers that vary greatly in size and color. For more than a century, in fact, growers have selected and marketed new gladioli, and today it is not easy to make a simple and clear classification of all existing hybrids. The following are the best known.

Large-flowered hybrids are up to 3–4 ft (1–1.2 m) tall, with dense spikes of 16–20 in (40–50 cm), comprising numerous flowers 6–7 in (15–18 cm) across. They come in a vast range of colors, with or without a throat, and with contrasted margins or markings.

Primulinus hybrids are 20–36 in (50–90 cm) tall, with thin spikes of 16–20 in (40–50 cm), comprising flower heads 3 in (7–8 cm) across, more loosely arranged, with a hooded top petal, delicate and in a very wide range of colors, usually quite pale.

Butterfly hybrids are 4–6 ft (1.2–1.8 m) tall, with spikes of 18 in (45 cm) composed of flowers $2^1/_2$–4 in (6–10 cm) across, generally yellow, orange or red, with contrasting margins and conspicuous spots on throat.

Miniature hybrids are a maximum 30 in (75 cm) tall, with dense spikes of 12–14 in (30–35 cm), comprising flowers of $1^1/_2$–2 in (4–5 cm), often ruffled, in bright colors, sometimes spotted and streaked.

G. × colvillei hybrids, probably the first gladiolus hybrids cultivated, are 18–24 in (45–60 cm) tall, with spikes of 10 in (25 cm), comprising flowers of 3 in (8 cm), scarlet with yellow streaks on lower petals.

Flowering period Summer.

Cultivation Relatively simple to grow, gladioli need a position in full sun and in light soil that is rich in organic material. Plant corms after last spring frost 4 in (10 cm) deep and 4–6 in (10–15 cm) apart. For prolonged flowering stagger planting at intervals of 10 days between mid spring and midsummer. During the entire growing period water regularly and plentifully. Moderate feeding is also advisable. Large-flowered gladioli should be supported by stakes. They are attacked by many pests and diseases, including aphids, red spider, nematodes, corm rot, gladiolus dry rot, rust, gladiolus fusarium wilt, and bacterial and virus infections.

Propagation In spring by cormels that form around adult corm.

Care Lift corms from ground after first frost, dry quickly in a warm place, clean off soil, treat with fungicide and insecticide, and keep sheltered from cold in airy position.

82 GLADIOLUS BYZANTINUM

Family Iridaceae.
Origin Mediterranean coasts.
Description Corm $^1/_2$–$^3/_4$in (1–2cm) in diameter, thin at top, upright, glabrous, cylindrical stem; linear, sharp, sword-like leaves; one-sided flowers in spikes with slightly zigzag axis; perigonium of $1^1/_4$–$2^1/_2$in (3–6cm), very deep purple with purple-bordered white central blotch.
Flowering period March–June.
Cultivation This large European gladiolus, which grows wild in fields of grain, likes dry, sandy soil enriched with manure, and sunny positions. Plant bulbs in late spring 6in (15cm) deep.
Propagation By cormels that form alongside principal corm.
Care In mild climates the bulbs may be left in the ground throughout the year without special care. Elsewhere, dig up in the autumn and replant in the spring.

---

83 GLADIOLUS TRISTIS

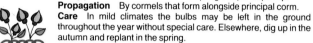

Family Iridaceae.
Origin Southern Africa.
Description Upright stem 18–24in (45–60cm) tall, very soft leaves, loose spikes of 8–10in (20–25cm) comprising stellate flowers of 2–3in (5–8cm), with fairly narrow petals, pale yellow or cream, which open toward evening. It is one of the few gladioli to have scented flowers. It has originated many horticultural hybrids.
Flowering period Spring.
Cultivation A fairly hardy species that requires, like all other gladioli, a position in full sun. Plant bulbs in autumn 4in (10cm) deep in fertile, permeable soil. Water regularly and feed moderately throughout growing period.
Propagation By cormels that form alongside the corm.
Care It is one of the species most resistant to cold and can therefore be left in the ground all winter without problem.

84 GLORIOSA ROTHSCHILDIANA
Glory lily, climbing lily   **U.S. zone 10**

Family Liliaceae.
Origin Tropical Africa.
Description Large, smooth, delicate white tubers, surrounded by a scaly brown tunic; slender, twining stem up to 7 ft (2 m) long; oval, lanceolate leaves, terminating in a tendril, which is used by the plant for attachment to a support; very showy flowers, 3–4 in (8–10 cm) across, with upward-curving petals, bright yellow and scarlet.
Flowering period Summer.
Cultivation This tender plant can be grown outside only in warmest regions. Plant tubers in pots, under glass, in spring, at 61°–65°F (16°–18°C), in a mixture of soil, sand and peat, with a little manure added (or use a good proprietary potting compost). Water abundantly during entire growth period and feed every fortnight until flowering. Give the plant a suitable support. During summer avoid direct sunlight.
Propagation By division of tubers in spring or from seed, with flowers after 4 years.
Care In all areas except U.S. zone 10, carefully dig up tubers in autumn, when leaves begin to fade, and keep them until spring in a cool, dry spot.
Other species *G. superba*.

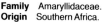

85 HAEMANTHUS ALBIFLOS
    U.S. zone 10

Family Amaryllidaceae.
Origin Southern Africa.
Description Good-sized bulb; large fleshy leaves about 8 in (20 cm) long, hairy at margins, appearing at time of flowering; scape 10 in (25 cm) tall, terminating in umbel of small tubular white flowers, with white bracts from which the stamens emerge.
Flowering period June.
Cultivation The species is not hardy and should be planted outdoors only in U.S. zone 10. Elsewhere, grow it in pots, indoors or in greenhouse. Plant bulbs just below surface in a mixture of soil, peat, and sand (or use a good proprietary potting compost). It prefers a sunny position. During the growth period the plant should be watered and fed regularly with liquid fertilizer. In summer, the rest period, watering and feeding should be completely stopped.
Propagation By very careful division of bulbs during rest period.
Care The bulb, which has many fleshy roots, is highly sensitive to transplanting and should therefore be left for as long as possible undisturbed.

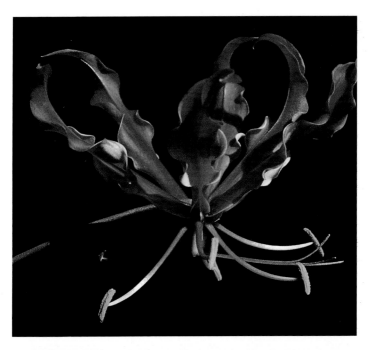

86 HAEMANTHUS COCCINEUS
Blood lily   U.S. zone 10

Family Amaryllidaceae.
Origin Southern Africa.
Description This is the most spectacular species of the genus. The bulb is about 3 in (7 cm) in diameter. The leaves, 20 in (50 cm) long and 6 in (15 cm) wide, appear after flowering. The scape is fleshy, spotted red, about 8 in (20 cm) tall and terminating in an umbel 6 in (15 cm) across. This is composed of numerous tubular coral-red flowers from which the stamens emerge. The bracts, also red, are very big and enclose the entire inflorescence.
Flowering period August–September.
Cultivation This can be grown outdoors in U.S. zone 10, but in colder areas plant it in pots indoors or in greenhouse. Set bulbs just below surface in a mixture of soil, sand, and peat. It prefers a sunny position. During the growing period water and feed regularly with liquid fertilizer.
Propagation By careful division of bulbs in rest period.
Care The bulb, which has many fleshy roots, is highly sensitive to transplanting and should therefore be left for as long as possible undisturbed.

87 HEDYCHIUM GARDNERIANUM
Ginger lily   U.S. zone 10

Family Zingiberaceae.
Origin India.
Description Plant up to 7 ft (2 m) tall, with a strong, creeping rhizome, an upright stem, lanceolate leaves 12 in (30 cm) long and wide, and spikes of tubular, scented flowers, 2 in (5 cm) across, yellow with deep scarlet stamens.
Flowering period Summer.
Cultivation The species is susceptible to frost and can survive outside only in very mild climates (U.S. zone 10). It is suitable for growing in pots indoors or in the greenhouse. Plant rhizomes under glass in spring in large pots which can be taken outside and placed in a warm, sunny position during the summer. Feed fortnightly with liquid fertilizer during growth period.
Propagation In spring, by division of rhizomes, after leaving the plant undisturbed for at least 3 years.
Care In autumn cut stems almost to ground level and return pots to greenhouse. Suspend watering completely during winter to let the plant rest.
Other species *H. coccineus, H. coronarium, H. flavum, H. greenei, H. spicatum.*

88 HELIANTHUS TUBEROSUS
Jerusalem artichoke   U.S. zone 4

Family Compositae.
Origin North America.
Description Rhizome 1–2 in (3–5 cm) across. Upright stem, up to 12 ft (3.6 m) tall; upper leaves alternate, 4–8 in (10–20 cm) long, oval-lanceolate with dentate margins, dark green above, rough to the touch. Bright yellow ligulate flowers are 3 in (7.6 cm) across.
Flowering period August–October.

Cultivation The Jerusalem artichoke is generally grown for its edible rhizome, which is dug up annually in autumn. It is useful, however, as a quick cover for waste ground, embankments, walls, etc. This species has few special needs and quickly spreads and becomes a weed unless restrained. It grows wild along rivers and streams and over wasteland, sometimes in very large numbers. Plant rhizomes in spring.
Propagation By division of rhizomes in autumn or spring.
Care Rhizomes can remain in the ground over winter, even in cold climates, without any problems.

---

89 HERMODACTYLUS TUBEROSUS
(Syn. *Iris tuberosa*)   U.S. zone 8
Snake's-head iris, Widow iris

Family Iridaceae.
Origin Southern coasts of Europe from Spain to Greece.
Description Tuberous plant with cylindrical upright stem, 12 in (30 cm) tall; linear leaves, quadrangular in section; single 2-in (5-cm) flowers enfolded at base by lanceolate spathe. Outer petals brown with pale edge; inner petals upright, yellowish-green.
Flowering period March–April.

Cultivation Cultivated for two or three centuries, this member of the iris family dislikes the cold and can therefore survive unprotected in the open only on warm, sheltered sites. It will, however, overwinter satisfactorily in most parts of Britain. It grows well in pots even in unheated places. Plant tubers at the end of summer just below surface in rich, loose, very well-drained, preferably alkaline soil.

Propagation By division of tubers after flowering.
Care In cold climates it is necessary to protect roots in winter, or raise plants in greenhouse.

90 HIPPEASTRUM Dutch hybrids
Amaryllis

Family Amaryllidaceae.
Origin Derived from species such as *H. vittatum* from the Peruvian Andes.
Description The typical form has a large bulb which produces a stem 20–30 in (50–75 cm) tall. The open trumpet-shaped flowers, 6 in (15 cm) across, come in a vast color range from white to pink, salmon and red, uniform or striped. Among the popular varieties are 'American Express,' with scarlet-crimson flowers, 'Bouquet,' salmon-pink, and 'Prima Donna,' crimson.
Flowering period Early winter to late spring. For early flowering.
Cultivation Extremely sensitive to frost, *Hippeastrum* only survives outside in U.S. zone 10 (not in Britain), in partial shade and in very fertile, moist soil. Otherwise it can be grown in pots, indoors or in the greenhouse. Plant bulbs in autumn or winter in a mixture of equal parts peat, humus, and sand, or any good potting compost. Water regularly and feed monthly until the plant is ready to rest. Suspend both during early autumn, when the plant rests.
Propagation In spring by division of small bulbs which form alongside bigger ones.
Care Keep pots indoors or in greenhouse during winter without applying any water or fertilizer until plant growth resumes.

---

91 HOMERIA COLLINA
(Syn. *H. breyniana*)

Family Iridaceae.
Origin Southern Africa.
Description Flattened corm; stem 20–24 in (50–60 cm) tall; thin linear leaves; open cup-shaped flowers 2$\frac{1}{2}$–3$\frac{1}{4}$ in (6–8 cm) across, orange with lighter yellow center. *Aurantiaca* has orange-red flowers with yellow center; *ochroleuca* (also known as *H. ochroleuca*) is bright yellow.
Flowering period Summer.
Cultivation The plant is normally grown in pots or outside in mild climates, in a sheltered, very sunny position. Not normally grown outside in Britain. Plant corms in autumn in mixture of equal parts peat, sand and humus. Place pots in a very well-lit spot. Water plentifully in spring until flowers appear; then suspend to induce the plant to rest.
Propagation By separating cormels in autumn, or from seed under glass.
Care If outside, protect ground during cold winters with a good mulch.

92 HYACINTHUS ORIENTALIS
Hyacinth

U.S. zone 6

Family   Liliaceae.

Origin   Eastern Mediterranean.

Description   Plant 10–12 in (25–30 cm) tall, with large bulb, stout, often grooved, linear leaves. The funnel-shaped flowers, 1 in (2.5 cm) wide, of waxy consistency and fragrant, are grouped in dense inflorescences of 6 in (15 cm) and borne on a strong, fleshy, upright scape.

This species, which is seldom grown, has originated a very large number of hybrids with single or double flowers, in colors ranging from blue and white to yellow and pink.

Varieties include 'Amsterdam,' salmon-red, 'Amethyst,' amethyst-blue, 'Bismarck,' light blue, 'Blue Giant,' blue, 'Carnegie,' white, 'Lady Derby,' pale pink, 'Orange Boven,' salmon-orange, 'Tubergen's Scarlet,' deep violet-red, etc.

Flowering period   Spring, or winter if forced indoors.

Cultivation   Hyacinths need a sunny position in light, sandy, very well-drained soil that has not recently been manured. Plant bulbs September–October 5–6 in (12–15 cm) deep. Suspend watering, which in any case should be moderate, after flowering.

To grow hyacinths indoors, pot them in autumn in light, sandy or proprietary peat-based compost (or bulb fiber if you are using a bowl without drainage), then keep for about 2 months in a cold, dark place, at a temperature of around 39°F (4°C), making sure the compost is kept fairly moist. When the roots are properly developed, move the pots into the light, initially at a temperature of 50°F (10°C), shifting them to a warmer position only after the inflorescences appear.

Hyacinths are likely to be attacked by nematodes, molds, and bacteria. Flowers may also drop prematurely as a result of a fall in temperature or humidity. If plants are forced too early, green flower petals may appear.

Propagation   From seed or bulblets, but actually it is best to buy new bulbs.

Care   To keep outdoor hyacinths in good condition lift bulbs from the ground after leaves have turned yellow, keep them throughout the summer in a dry place and replant them in autumn. A light mulch in winter is advisable. The plant tends as a rule to produce new but increasingly smaller flowers each year, so it is best to purchase new bulbs every 3–4 years. Bulbs used indoors are best planted in the garden after flowering.

93 HYMENOCALLIS × FESTALIS

Family   Amaryllidaceae.
Origin   Hybrid of horticultural origin.
Description   This hybrid of *H. longipetala* and *H. narcissiflora* has a large bulb, linear leaves 12 in (30 cm) long, and a stem of 16–18 in (40–45 cm) terminating in an umbel of 2–4 trumpet-shaped, scented flowers, 6 in (15 cm) across. The flowers are white with a central trumpet and characteristic long, narrow, outward-curving outer petals.
Flowering period   Midsummer.
Cultivation   This delicate plant can be grown outside only in warm, sunny positions. It also grows well in pots. Plant bulbs in spring 6 in (15 cm) deep in well-drained, humus-rich soil; if potted, use a mixture of equal parts soil, sand, and peat. Feed every 2–3 weeks and water abundantly until flowering.
Propagation   By division of bulbs during rest period.
Care   At the first sign of cold lift bulbs from ground and keep them throughout winter in pots of peat at temperature of 50°–59°F (10°–15°C). Pots can be kept in greenhouse or taken indoors.

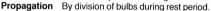

94 HYMENOCALLIS NARCISSIFLORA

(Syn. *Ismene calathina, Hymenocallis calathina*)   U.S. zone 8
Peruvian daffodil, Basket flower

Family   Amaryllidaceae.
Origin   Peru.
Description   Plant with large bulb, very decorative linear leaves 12 in (30 cm) long, flower scape of 20–28 in (50–70 cm) terminating in umbel of 5 highly scented flowers, white with green stripes, with a central trumpet and characteristic long, narrow, outward-curving outer petals.
Flowering period   Early summer.
Cultivation   Introduced into Europe toward the end of the eighteenth century, this is the best-known species of the genus, grown on a large scale in northern Europe for cut flowers. Normally grown in pots, it survives in the open only in warmest areas (not in Britain), in warm, sunny positions. Plant bulbs in spring 6 in (15 cm) deep in well-drained, humus-rich soil; if potted, use a mixture of equal parts soil, sand and peat, or any good proprietary potting compost. Feed every 2–3 weeks and water abundantly until flowering.
Propagation   By removing small offset bulbs during rest period.
Care   In colder zones, lift bulbs in the autumn and keep them throughout winter in pots of peat at temperature of 50°–59°F (10°–15°C). Pots can be kept in greenhouse or taken indoors.

95 IPHEION UNIFLORUM

(Syn. *Triteleia uniflora, Brodiaea uniflora*) **U.S. zone 6**
Spring star flower

Family Liliaceae.
Origin Peru, Argentina.
Description Small bulbous plant, about 8 in (20 cm) tall, with wiry leaves that smell of onions, stems terminating in stellate, single, scented flowers, white or blue-violet, about 1¼ in (3 cm) wide. Cultivated varieties include 'Caeruleum,' with light blue flowers, and 'Wisley Blue,' blue-violet.
Flowering period Spring.
Cultivation A fairly hardy species, it does well outside in temperate climates. Plant bulbs in autumn 4 in (10 cm) deep and 6 in (15 cm) apart, in sunny position or partial shade, and in well-drained soil. No special care is necessary.
Propagation The bulbs multiply on their own very rapidly. Remove them from ground every 2–3 years in midsummer and transplant them, taking care not to damage them.
Care Protect ground in winter with a light mulch to avoid damage from cold.

96 IRIS

Iris **U.S. zone 5 (but not all types)**

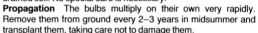

Family Iridaceae.
Origin Europe, Asia and America, with hybrids of horticultural origin.
Description There are more than 200 species belonging to the genus *Iris*, and a large number of horticultural hybrids. In the majority of cases, they have sword-shaped leaves, arranged fanwise, and flowers with a perigonium formed of two series of segments, joined at the base. The three outer segments, wide at the tip and narrow at the base, are turned backward, while the three inner segments are upright.

   This vast genus is normally subdivided into groups and sections based on certain evident morphological features. One essential distinction is between rhizomatous irises and bulbous irises. The former, in their turn, comprise three sections: bearded irises (Pogoniris), beardless irises (Apogon) and crested irises (Evansia). The bulbous irises, on the other hand, contain only one section. The individual sections, except for the crested irises, are further subdivided into subsections and groups, of which we shall mention only the principal ones.

BEARDED IRISES (POGONIRIS)
There are many bearded iris species and hybrids. Their flowers are characterized by a beard of fleshy hairs on the three outer

petals. These petals, arranged horizontally, are known as wings, while the three inner petals, upright, are called standards. The gray-green, sword-shaped leaves form fans. Bearded irises are subdivided into Arillata, with an aril around the seed tegument, and Eupogon, which are bearded.

The subsection Eupogon contains: *Iris germanica*, generally violet with a white beard; *I. florentina* (correctly *I. germanica florentina*), with bluish-white flowers and rhizomes which, when dried and ground, are used in perfumery; and *I. pallida*, with highly ornamental leaves in the forms 'Aureo-variegata' and 'Argenteo-variegata.' In addition, there are hybrids in all colors.

The Arillata irises are subdivided into the Oncocyclus group, which comprises *I. susiana*, originally from Turkey and cultivated in Europe since 1572, creamy-white with dark purple veins and streaks, and *I. gatesii*, with silver-white flowers and purple veining; and the Regelia group, which consists of *I. stolonifera*, with bronze and blue flowers, and *I. hoogiana*, with lavender-blue flowers.

BEARDLESS IRISES (APOGON)

This section is made up of plants with very elegant flowers, often bicolored, delicately streaked, and with smooth, not bearded, outer petals. The leaves, as a rule, are persistent, linear, and fairly narrow. There are six principal groups, five of which are listed below.

The Californica group comprises numerous hybrids and species of North American origin, with delicate flowers, $2^3/_4-3^1/_4$ in (7–8 cm) wide, suitable for cutting, and with dark green leaves. The group includes *I. douglasiana*, *I. innominata*, *I. tenax*, and many hybrids of different colors.

The Hexagona group consists of plants with zigzag stems and narrow, evergreen leaves. The flowers are 4–6 in (10–15 cm) in diameter. The fruits are capsules with six characteristic ribs. The group includes *I. brevicaulis*, with purple-blue flowers, *I. fulva* and, among hybrids, the variety 'Dixie Deb.'

The Laevigatae group is made up typically of species that grow in swampy zones and on the shores of lakes, rivers and streams. It includes *I. pseudacorus*, with yellow flowers, *I. versicolor* and *I. laevigata*.

The Sibiricae group comprises species with herbaceous, filiform leaves and slender stems that bear flowers $2^1/_2-4$ in (6–10 cm) in diameter. It includes *I. sibirica*, a typical species of meadows and wet woodlands, and *I. chrysographes*.

The Spuria group consists of hardy tufted irises with sturdy glaucous leaves and flowers $2^1/_2-6$ in (6–15 cm) in diameter. The fruits are capsules, with a characteristic double ribbing. The group includes *I. graminea*, with violet flowers, often found in woodland clearings; *I. spuria*, with purple-blue flowers; and numerous hybrids of different colors.

CRESTED IRISES (EVANSIA)

The crested irises include diverse species, varieties and hybrids with delicate, softly colored flowers, characterized by a conspicuous fringed crest on the outer petals. The smallest species, 6 in (15 cm) tall, are suitable for the rock garden. The section includes *I. cristata*, originally from North America, represented by varieties with white or lavender flowers; *I. japonica*, with lilac, yellow-spotted flowers; and *I. confusa*, with white, mauve-flushed flowers.

BULBOUS IRISES

This section is made up of all the irises that grow from bulbs. As a rule these are subdivided into the groups Juno, Reticulata and Xiphium.

The irises of the Juno group, originally from Central Asia, have bulbs furnished with fleshy, tuberous roots. The stems are upright;

the leaves, gray-green below, are short-lived; and there are 4–8 flowers measuring 3¼ in (8 cm) across on each stem. Representative species are *I. bucharica*, 18 in (45 cm) tall, with white and golden-yellow petals, and *I. magnifica*, 24 in (60 cm) tall, with pale lilac flowers.

The irises of the Reticulata group are small in size and have bulbs with a fibrous tunic, pointed leaves and very early flowers of 2–3¼ in (5–8 cm) diameter. The most common species are *I. reticulata* which, since its introduction from Asia in 1865, has originated numerous horticultural varieties with very beautiful purple-blue flowers; *I. danfordiae*, only 2–2¾ in (5–7 cm) tall, with lemon-yellow flowers; and *I. bakeriana*, with three mauve inner petals and three violet-blue outer petals, streaked white and violet with a large black spot.

The irises of the Xiphium group are 12–24 in (30–60 cm) tall and comprise several of the most important horticultural irises. These include *I. xiphium*, which grows wild in southwestern Europe, with violet, yellow-striped flowers, and *I. xiphioides*, known as the English iris although it came originally from Spain, with large blue flowers.

Flowering period Bearded irises flower in late spring. The Californica, Laevigatae and Spuria groups of non-bearded irises flower in spring. The Hexagona and Sibirica groups of non-bearded irises flower in summer. Crested irises flower in late spring. The Reticulata group of bulbous irises flower January–March, and the Juno and Xiphium groups in spring.

Cultivation The various groups require different treatment, as follows:

BEARDED IRISES
The Arillata, especially the Oncocyclus group, are extremely sensitive and every gardener derives satisfaction from growing them successfully. These plants are particularly allergic to wet soil and standing water. Plant the rhizomes in late autumn in a sunny position 2 in (5 cm) deep, in calcareous soil with a later addition of bonemeal, and thoroughly drained. After the flowering period it is sensible to cover the ground with panes of glass to protect the rhizomes and encourage them to develop. The Eupogon irises, on the other hand, are extremely hardy and require a position in full sun and well-drained soil. Plant the rhizomes end summer to early autumn, allowing the upper part to protrude. The dwarf varieties are highly suitable for the rock garden.

NON-BEARDED IRISES
The majority of non-bearded irises need neutral, moist soil and a position in full sun. Those of the Spuria group are the hardiest, suited to any ground. Plant the rhizomes 1–2 in (2.5–5 cm) deep or, in the case of aquatic irises, bury them to a depth of ½–¾ in (1–2 cm) in places where the water is 4–6 in (10–15 cm) deep.

CRESTED IRISES
These need fertile, humus-rich, non-calcareous soil, and a partly shaded position. Plant the rhizomes in early spring, just below ground level.

BULBOUS IRISES
The irises of the Reticulata group are especially popular for early flowering (January–March). They need a warm position in full sun and calcareous, sandy, thoroughly drained soil. Their small size makes them ideal for the rock garden. Plant the bulbs in autumn, 2–3 in (5–8 cm) deep, directly in the ground or in pots as house plants.

The irises of the Juno group are, with the exception of certain species like *I. bucharica*, difficult to grow, needing a sheltered position in full sun. The bulbs need very careful handling to avoid damaging the roots, and should be planted in early autumn 5 in

(12cm) deep and 6in (15cm) apart in light, well-drained soil.

The irises of the Xiphium group do not as a rule present any problems of cultivation. Plant the bulbs in autumn about 4in (10cm) deep.

All irises are likely to be attacked by various pests and diseases, including aphids, nematodes, iris rhizome rot, rust, sclerosis, and cucumber mosaic virus, which affects rhizomatous irises, forming chlorotic spots and streaks on the leaves and flowers.

Propagation Bearded irises, by division of rhizomes in autumn. Beardless irises, by division of rhizomes in early autumn or early spring, taking care to keep the ground moist for some days after transplanting. Irises of the Californica group also reproduce easily from seed. Crested irises, every two years, after flowering, by digging up the rhizomes and dividing them. Bulbous irises, by division of the bulbs in early autumn. Handle them carefully and replant them immediately. The irises of the Juno group multiply very slowly.

Care The rhizomes of bearded irises should be removed from the ground only to be divided. The irises of the very delicate Oncocyclus group should be provided with ground protection after flowering to prevent damage from excessive wetness. The rhizomes of beardless irises should be left undisturbed in the ground. Irises of the Hexagona group should be protected in winter with a layer of straw or leaves. Among the crested irises, *I. japonica* is the most sensitive to cold and the ground should therefore be protected with straw or leaves. The bulbs of all bulbous irises can be left undisturbed in the ground for 3–5 years.

97 IXIA VIRIDIFLORA

U.S. zone 9

Family Iridaceae.
Origin Southern Africa.
Description Small corm with stem 12–16 in (30–40 cm) tall; linear, sword-shaped leaves; panicles of six-petaled flowers of an unusual electric blue-green color, 1¼ in (3 cm) across. This species has given rise to a large number of hybrids, up to 24 in (60 cm) tall, with yellow, red, purple, and blue flowers. They include 'Afterglow,' orange-brown with dark center; 'Bridesmaid,' white; 'Hogarth,' yellow with darker center, though in Britain they are almost always sold as mixtures.
Flowering period Late spring, summer.
Cultivation The plants are sensitive to frost, growing well in pots or outside only in a mild climate and in a sunny, well-sheltered position. Plant the corms in late autumn in a mixture of equal parts peat, sand, and soil. Pots indoors should be set in a very well-lit position, perhaps on a windowsill, in a cool room at 44°–50°F (7°–10°C). Water plentifully during spring until the plants flower.
Propagation By separating the cormels in autumn or from seed, with flowers after 3 years.
Care After flowering, the corms should be removed from the soil and kept dry over the summer. Outside, protect the ground from winter cold with a generous mulch.

---

98 IXIOLIRION MONTANUM
(Syn. *I. pallasii, I. tataricum*)

U.S. zone 8

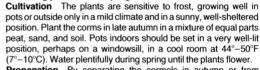

Family Amaryllidaceae.
Origin Central and western Asia.
Description Elegant plant with small ovoid bulb; long, slender, linear leaves that appear in spring before the flowers; stem up to 16 in (40 cm) tall, terminating in a raceme of six-petaled tubular flowers, lavender-blue, about 2 in (5 cm) wide, delicately scented.
Flowering period Late spring.
Cultivation Originally from the steppes of Central Asia, this species needs a well-drained soil and a warm, sheltered position in full sun. Plant the bulbs in autumn 4 in (10 cm) deep and 6 in (15 cm) apart. No feeding is necessary.
Propagation By separating bulblets in autumn, after the aerial part of the plant is dry, or in spring from seed in greenhouse.
Care Remove bulbs from ground in autumn and keep over winter in dry peat at 50°–59°F (10°–15°C).

99 LACHENALIA ALOIDES
(Syn. *L. tricolor*) U.S. zone 9
Cape cowslip

Family Liliaceae.
Origin Southern Africa.
Description Small plant with spherical bulb, linear leaves light green, often spotted or striped violet, stem 8–12 in (20–30 cm) tall, terminating in racemes of about 20 tubular, pendulous flowers, $^3/_4$–$1^1/_4$ in (2–3 cm) long, usually yellow with green or orange spots. The variety 'Aurea' has orange-yellow flowers; 'Lutea,' deep yellow flowers.
Flowering period Late winter–early spring.
Cultivation This species is highly sensitive to frost and is usually raised indoors or in the greenhouse. Plant bulbs in September, in a pot, using a mixture of equal parts sand, peat and soil, or any good potting compost. Water and keep dry through winter in a cool greenhouse or a well-lit spot protected from cold. As soon as the flower scapes appear, bring pots indoors. If the temperature is not too high, prolonged flowering is possible. During the entire growing period water and feed every fortnight. Reduce water after flowering and suspend altogether during summer to allow a rest period for the bulbs.
Propagation By separating the bulblets in summer.
Care In winter leave the bulbs in pots in the cold house.

100 LACHENALIA BULBIFERA
(Syn. *L. pendula*) U.S. zone 9

Family Liliaceae.
Origin Southern Africa.
Description A similar plant to the previous species, this has a spherical bulb, two large leaves and a strong stem terminating in racemes of about 10 tubular, pendulous flowers, 1–$1^1/_4$ in (2.5–3 cm) long, dark purple, yellow or red.
Flowering period Mid winter.
Cultivation This species is generally grown indoors or in the greenhouse. Plant 5–7 bulbs in August in a large bowl, using a mixture of equal parts sand, peat, and soil, or any good potting compost. Water and keep dry through winter in a cool greenhouse or well-lit spot protected from frost. Bring indoors as soon as flower scapes appear. Prolonged flowering from mid winter onward may be obtained if temperature is not too high. During entire growing period water and feed fortnightly. Gradually reduce water after flowering and suspend completely during the summer to allow bulbs a rest period.
Propagation By separating bulblets in summer.
Care Leave the bulbs in pots in a cool greenhouse over summer.

101 LAPEIROUSIA LAXA

(Syn. *Anomatheca cruenta*)

U.S. zone 9

Family Iridaceae.
Origin Southern Africa.
Description Plant 10–12 in (25–30 cm) tall, with flattened corm protected by a tunic; linear, sword-shaped leaves; and one-sided spikes of 10–12 stellate red flowers 1 in (2.5 cm) across.
Flowering period Summer.
Cultivation This species is suitable for growing outdoors only in temperate-hot climates, where it needs a sunny position, partial shade, and very well-drained soil. Plant corms in March 2 in (5 cm) deep. The plant can also be grown in pots in the cool greenhouse and brought indoors when about to flower. In this case plant corms in autumn in groups of 7–8 to the container. Use a mixture of equal parts sand, peat, and soil, or any good potting compost. Water moderately at first and then more plentifully until flowering, and feed fortnightly. Suspend both operations during summer when growth is complete.
Propagation By separating the cormels from the larger corms, or from seed.
Care In autumn lift corms from ground and overwinter in a dry, cold place.

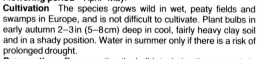

102 LEUCOJUM AESTIVUM

Summer snowflake

U.S. zone 4

Family Amaryllidaceae.
Origin Europe and Caucasus.
Description Pear-shaped bulb with light brown tunic; linear leaves, all basal; trigonal scape, 14–20 in (35–50 cm); umbels of 2–8 pendulous flowers, 6 in (15 cm) across, wrapped in a membranous spathe, with white petals spotted green at tip. 'Gravetye Giant' is the sturdiest of the varieties.
Flowering period April–May.
Cultivation The species grows wild in wet, peaty fields and swamps in Europe, and is not difficult to cultivate. Plant bulbs in early autumn 2–3 in (5–8 cm) deep in cool, fairly heavy clay soil and in a shady position. Water in summer only if there is a risk of prolonged drought.
Propagation By separating the bulblets during the rest period.
Care Leave the bulbs undisturbed in ground for several years prior to separating bulblets. No winter protection is necessary.

103 LEUCOJUM VERNUM
Spring snowflake   U.S. zone 4

Family Amaryllidaceae.
Origin Warm regions of Europe.
Description Similar to *L. aestivum*, this species is somewhat smaller – 8–12 in (20–30 cm) tall, with linear leaves shorter than the scape, dark green, partly developed at time of flowering. The stem is double-edged, terminating in one or two $^5/_8$–1 in (15–25 mm) flowers with white petals green-spotted at tip. These are enfolded at the base in a membranous spathe. 'Carpathicum' has yellow-tipped petals.
Flowering period February–April.
Cultivation The plant grows wild in wet woodlands, alongside ditches, and on peaty ground, forming attractive carpets in mid and late winter. Sometimes confused with the snowdrop, the spring snowflake is easy to cultivate. Plant the bulbs at the end of summer 2–3 in (5–8 cm) deep in cool soil and a fairly shady position. No special care is necessary.
Propagation By separating the bulblets during the rest period.
Care Leave bulbs undisturbed in ground for several years before separating them. No winter protection is necessary.

Leocojum vernum 'Carpathicum.'

104 LILIUM
Lily   U.S. zone 3 (but not all kinds)

Family Liliaceae.
Origin America, Europe, Asia and hybrids of horticultural origin.
Description Long admired for their aesthetic qualities and often depicted as symbols of purity and regality, lilies are among the most loved and popular bulbous plants. They generally have bulbs with loose scales that are not enclosed in a protective tunic; upright, leafy stems; short, lanceolate leaves; and flowers either single or in loose racemes made up of six petals of all colors except blue. They are often spotted. The male reproductive organs are composed of six stamens, while the pistil is trilobed at the tip. The fruit is a capsule with many seeds. Some species and varieties, known as stem-rooters, also have characteristic of putting out roots from the stem above the bulb, which means they should be planted deep enough for the stem roots to develop adequately. Others are basal-rooters, like most bulbs.
  Lilies are classified, on the basis of their origin, form, and position of flowers, into nine divisions, the last of which is composed of botanical species.
  Asiatic hybrids (group 1). Plants that flower early (June), up to 5 ft (1.5 m) tall, with flowers 4–6 in (10–15 cm) across, in colors ranging from red to yellow and creamy-white, curving upward, inward or pendulous. 'Mid-Century' hybrids have upright flowers

Lilium, Asiatic hybrid (group 1).

that either curve outward or are pendulous; they are lemon-yellow, orange, crimson or red, streaked with brown, 4–5 in (10–13 cm) across, single or in umbels.

Martagon hybrids (group 2). Derived from *Lilium hansonii* and *L. martagon*, they are 5–6 ft (1.5–1.8 m) tall, in variable colors, generally spotted, recurved, pendulous, in racemes of 20–30 elements. They include the 'Backhouse' and 'Paisley' hybrids.

Candidum hybrids (group 3). Derived from crosses of *L. candidum* and other European species, they are up to 6 ft (1.8 m) tall and have scented flowers with backward-bending petals, 3–4 in (7–10 cm) across, in variable colors, with deep red pollen. One of the oldest garden hybrids, *L.* × *testaceum*, has pendulous flowers with retroflex petals, yellow with red anthers.

American hybrids (group 4). Derived from crosses of various American species, they are 4–8 ft (1.2–2.4 m) tall. The 'Bellingham' hybrids are 5–6¹/₂ ft (1.5–2 m) tall, with recurved flowers, orange-yellow, red or bicolored, spotted brown, 2–3 in (5–7 cm) across.

Longiflorum hybrids (group 5). Derived from *L. longiflorum* and *L. formosanum*, they have horizontal, trumpet-shaped flowers. They are very prone to viral diseases and are rarely cultivated.

Trumpet-shaped and Aurelian hybrids (group 6). Derived from Asiatic species, they are 4–6 ft (1.2–1.8 m) tall. In their turn they are subdivided, according to flower shape, into four subgroups: trumpet-shaped flowers ('Green Emerald,' 'Limelight'), cup-shaped flowers ('First Love' and 'Heart's Desire'), pendent flowers and stellate flowers ('Bright Star' and 'Golden Sunburst' groups of hybrids).

Oriental hybrids (group 7). These are perhaps the loveliest of hybrids, with enormous, highly scented flowers, often white with golden, pink, and crimson streaks and spots. They are in their turn subdivided, according to flower shape, into four subgroups: trumpet-shaped flowers, cup-shaped flowers ('Empress of China,' 'Empress of India'), star-shaped flowers ('Imperial Crimson,' 'Imperial Gold'), and recurved flowers (like the hybrid 'Jamboree').

Various hybrids (group 8). All hybrids not classified in other groups.

True species (group 9). Botanical species and their forms. The principal botanical species that are grown are dealt with in the following entries, but other well-known ones are *L. auratum, L. canadense, L. dauricum, L. davidii, L. japonicum, L. pardalinum, L. pumilum* and *L. speciosum.*

Flowering period Mainly summer outdoors.

Cultivation In nature lilies grow exclusively in the northern hemisphere, between latitudes 11° and 16°, and in regions with alternating hot and cold, dry, and wet climates. In general they prefer temperate zones and in Asia appear as mountain plants. They need light, thoroughly drained soil and thus tend to colonize sloping ground where there is a minimum risk of standing water.

Growing lilies does not create special problems. They are mostly very hardy plants, resistant to winter frosts. Plant the bulbs outside in autumn or early spring, 6–8 in (15–20 cm) deep and 6–10 in (15–25 cm) apart. Species or hybrids that form roots on the collar of the stem should be planted 10 in (25 cm) deep. Basal-rooting lilies are generally best planted in autumn.

They require porous, well-drained soil with plenty of organic material, in full sun or, in the hottest areas, partial shade. The American hybrids in particular grow well in half-shade. They do not under any circumstances tolerate standing water. During the growing period it is advisable to feed in spring and summer. In

Lilium, trumpet-shaped hybrid (group 6).

autumn mulch with leafmold or garden compost, but do not use fresh manure.

The plants are always susceptible to pests and diseases. The bulbs may be eaten by squirrels and rodents in general, while slugs and snails, aphids, fungi, and viral diseases may attack the plants.

Lilies are also very beautiful as cut flowers, but it is worth remembering that if the plant is deprived of all or most of its leaves, in addition to flowers, it will not be able to accumulate the necessary food reserves and almost always dies.

Propagation In autumn by separating individual bulb scales; by separating the bulbils which, in some species, varieties and hybrids, form at the base of the stem or in the leaf axils; or from seed, with flowers after 4 years. During propagation, remember that lily bulbs are very delicate and are not protected by a tunic from temperature fluctuations and humidity. So they do not like to be transplanted and should be handled with care and replanted as soon as possible.

Care The bulbs survive outdoors throughout the year without problem.

Lilium 'Green Dragon,' trumpet-shaped hybrid (group 6).

105 LILIUM BULBIFERUM
Bulbil lily   **U.S. zone 3**

Family Liliaceae.
Origin Europe.
Description This lily grows to a height of 1¼–3 in (3–8 cm), has a small bulb of ¾ in (1.5 cm) with pointed white scales, an upright stem, spotted purple at the base, lanceolate leaves, the upper ones bearing a bulbil at the axil, and 1–5 flowers, open at the top, orange-yellow with brown spots. The variety *croceum* is also common, slightly taller and without bulbils.
Flowering period June–July.
Cultivation This beautiful lily, which grows wild in deciduous woods and subalpine meadows, is easy to cultivate and does well in all kinds of fertile, well-drained soil. Plant the bulbs in spring or autumn 3–4 in (8–10 cm) deep.
Propagation In autumn by the underground bulblets or the bulbils in the leaf axils.
Care The bulbs may be left in the ground throughout the year without protection.

106 LILIUM CANDIDUM
Madonna lily

Family   Liliaceae.
Origin   Eastern Mediterranean.
Description   This splendid lily, known since antiquity and often depicted as the symbol of purity, has a pear-shaped bulb with brown scales; an upright, cylindrical, glabrous stem; linear leaves up to 10 in (25 cm) long, tending to become smaller above; and racemes of 5–10 scented flowers, 3 in (7.6 cm) across, with pure white petals, revolute at the tip.
Flowering period   June–July.
Cultivation   The Madonna lily does well in calcium-rich soil and in bright positions. Plant the bulbs 1–2 in (2.5–5 cm) deep in August–September so that the leaves, which persist through the winter, have time to develop.
Propagation   In late summer by separating the bulblets that grow around the bulb. The plant very seldom produces seeds.
Care   The bulbs may be left in the ground throughout the year without protection.

---

107 LILIUM MARTAGON
Martagon lily, Turk's-cap lily

Family   Liliaceae.
Origin   Europe and Asia.
Description   The martagon lily has a large bulb, an upright, cylindrical stem, striped violet at the base, verticils of 4–8 lanceolate-spatulate leaves, and racemes of 6–20 pendulous, disagreeably smelling flowers, with purple-red, waxy, outward-curving petals. 'Album' has white flowers and 'Gleam' red, black-spotted flowers.
Flowering period   June–July.
Cultivation   This very widespread species, which grows wild in woods and fields at altitudes of 1,000–5,250 ft (300–1,600 m), does well in all types of soil, preferably slightly calcareous, and in partial shade. It tends to naturalize.
Propagation   In autumn by separating the bulblets that grow around the bulb or by separating the bulb scales. The seeds germinate easily but the plantlets need 7–8 years to flower.
Care   The bulbs may be left in the ground throughout the year without protection.

108 LILIUM REGALE
Regal lily U.S. zone 3

Family Liliaceae.
Origin Western China.
Description This famous, widespread lily, imported from China in 1903, has a medium-sized, scaly, yellow-white bulb, an upright stem up to 5 ft (1.5 m) tall, linear-lanceolate leaves, and racemes of delicately scented, funnel-shaped flowers, white with a yellow throat, flushed pink outside.
Flowering period June–July.
Cultivation The species is extremely adaptable and easy to grow, doing best in well-drained soil and a sunny position. Plant the bulbs in autumn about 3 in (7.6 cm) below the surface or more deeply, 6–8 in (15–20 cm), in very sandy soil.
Propagation By dividing the bulblets in autumn. The plant also reproduces freely from seed, but flowers only after 3 years.
Care In especially cold climates give a good mulch in winter.

109 LILIUM TIGRINUM
Tiger lily U.S. zone 3

Family Liliaceae.
Origin Eastern China, Japan.
Description The tiger lily has a large bulb, an upright, cylindrical stem with spider-web patterning and aerial bulbils, linear-lanceolate leaves, and racemes of 20–25 pendulous, retroflex, delicately scented, 4-in (10-cm) flowers, bright orange red with purple-black spots. The variety *flaviflorum* has bright yellow, purple-spotted flowers.
Flowering period Late summer and early autumn.
Cultivation Cultivated for centuries by the Chinese and Japanese as a food plant (the bulbs are edible), the tiger lily grows well in full sun and in neutral, fertile, well-drained soil. Plant the bulbs in autumn 6 in (15 cm) deep and 8 in (20 cm) apart. The species is particularly subject to virus disease.
Propagation In autumn by separating the bulbils. The flowers are often sterile.
Care In cold climates give a light mulch in winter.

110 MERENDERA MONTANA
(Syn. *M. bulbocodium*)

Family Liliaceae.
Origin Iberian peninsula.
Description Small plant not more than 2 in (5 cm) tall, closely related to the colchicum, with a small corm protected by a brown tunic, 3–4 slender linear leaves that appear just after flowering, 1–2 purple-pink or violet flowers, 1¼–2 in (3–5 cm) across, with separate petals and yellow anthers.
Flowering period Late summer–autumn.
Cultivation This elegant plant, which grows wild in the mountains of Spain and Portugal, is seldom cultivated and is ideal for the rock garden. It needs cool, sandy soil fortified with manure. Plant the corms in a sunny or half-shady position in July–August, after the leaves wither.
Propagation From seed in autumn or by growing on the small corms that form around the parent in late autumn.
Care The corms can be left in the ground during winter without problem.

111 MUSCARI ARMENIACUM
Grape hyacinth

Family Liliaceae.
Origin Asia Minor.
Description Plant 6–8 in (15–20 cm) tall with white bulb, narrow linear leaves, gray-green above, upright stems terminating in dense racemes of campanulate flowers, cobalt-blue with a white border, delicately scented. There are several horticultural varieties, including a double form.
Flowering period Spring.
Cultivation There are no special problems in growing the grape hyacinth. Plant bulbs at the end of summer or in early autumn, 4 in (10 cm) deep, in any kind of soil, in full sun. Do not feed. They tend to spread naturally and when, after a few years, they become too thick, it is advisable to uproot them. The cut flowers make an attractive, decorative display; if potted in early autumn in a mixture of equal parts peat, sand and soil, or any good potting compost, the grape hyacinth will flower in winter.
Propagation In autumn by dividing clumps of the bulbs, which should be replanted at once. The plant also spreads rapidly by self-seeding.
Care The bulbs survive in the ground over the winter without protection.

112 MUSCARI BOTYROIDES
Grape hyacinth U.S. zone 5

Family Liliaceae.
Origin Mediterranean Europe.
Description Slightly smaller plant than the previous one, with ovate, pear-shaped bulb. The upright leaves, 6–8 in (15–20 cm) tall, are characteristically spatulate, constituting a distinctive feature of the species. The small globose flowers, deep violet-blue with a white throat, are in loose racemes. 'Album,' with white flowers, is very beautiful.
Flowering period Spring.
Cultivation This grape hyacinth grows wild in fields and meadows of the Mediterranean region and, like the previous species, is easy to cultivate. It is very useful in the rock garden. Plant bulbs at the end of summer or in autumn, 4 in (10 cm) deep, in almost any kind of soil, in full sun. No feeding is necessary. They tend to spread naturally and after a few years, when too thick, should be thinned.
Propagation In autumn by dividing clumps, which should be replanted at once. The plant also spreads quickly through self-seeding.
Care The bulbs survive through the winter without need of protection.

---

113 MUSCARI MACROCARPUM
Grape hyacinth U.S. zone 6

Family Liliaceae.
Origin Greek islands and western Turkey.
Description This small grape hyacinth, 4–8 in (10–20 cm) tall, has a bulb with persistent fleshy roots, 2–6 linear green leaves, grooved and often recurved, dense racemes of yellow flowers with a brown throat, almost tubular, delicately scented.
Flowering period Spring.
Cultivation This very beautiful species is more sensitive to frost than the preceding two. Plant bulbs end of summer or in autumn, 4 in (10 cm) deep, in any kind of soil, in full sun or shady position. No feeding or watering are necessary.
Propagation In autumn by dividing bulbs, which should be replanted at once.
Care During winter the bulbs may be left outside but it is advisable to protect the ground with a mulch of leaves.

114 Genus NARCISSUS

Narcissus, daffodil, jonquil

Family Amaryllidaceae.
Origin Central Europe, North Africa. Horticultural hybrids and varieties.

Description These much-loved spring flowers have a pear-shaped bulb; linear, upright, flat, basal, glaucous-green leaves; an erect leafless scape, $2^{1}/_{2}$–24 in (6–60 cm) tall, depending on species and variety, that terminates in usually single, sometimes several flowers which, in bud, are enfolded by a green or papery spathe. Six petals, varying in color from white to orange, opening star-like, are joined at the base so as to form a central tube of variable length, known as the "cup" or "corona" if width exceeds length, or as the "trumpet" if length exceeds width. The fruit is a capsule. The bulbs are poisonous.

Narcissi and daffodils are normally divided, according to the origin and shape of the flowers, into eleven groups, the tenth of which is made up of wild species.

Trumpet daffodils (group 1). This group is so named because the flowers have a long trumpet. The plants are 16–20 in (40–50 cm) tall and have one flower per stem. The color combinations are yellow, yellow and white, white, and other shades of pale yellow and orange. The best-known varieties are 'King Alfred' and 'Golden Harvest.'

Large-cupped narcissi (group 2). These have a cup more than one-third as long as the segments of the perianth, but not longer. The plants are 16–18 in (40–45 cm) tall and have one flower per stem. Varieties include 'Carlton,' with entirely yellow flowers; 'Duke of Windsor,' white flowers with orange-yellow corona; and 'Flower Record,' white flowers with orange-yellow corona and darker margin.

Small-cupped narcissi (group 3). These are generally 14–18 in (35–45 cm) tall, with cups less than one-third the length of the perianth segments. 'Birma' has a yellow perianth and scarlet-orange corona; 'Barrett Browning' has a white perianth and orange corona.

Double narcissi (group 4). Varieties of this type, generally 14–18 in (35–45 cm) tall, have double flowers, with one or two flowers per stem. Among the best-known varieties are 'Golden Ducat,' with completely yellow flowers; 'Irene Copeland,' creamy-white and apricot-yellow flowers; and 'Texas,' with large yellow and orange flowers.

Triandrus narcissi (group 5). This group comprises narcissi derived from *Narcissus triandrus*, the pendulous flowers having a silky, outward-recurved perianth. The plants are 10–12 in (25–30 cm) tall, generally with several flowers per stem. Varieties include the long-cupped 'Liberty Bells' and 'Thalia' and the short-cupped 'Hawera.'

Cyclamineus narcissi (group 6). Derived from *N. cyclamineus*, these are 8–10 in (20–25 cm) tall, with pendulous flowers, similar to cyclamen, with a retroflex perianth and a long, narrow trumpet. The smallest varieties are ideal for the rock garden. They include 'February Gold,' with golden-yellow flowers; 'February Silver,' white flowers; and 'Jack Snipe,' creamy-white flowers with golden-yellow trumpet.

Above: trumpet daffodil (group 1).
Below: large-cupped narcissus (group 2).

(*continued overleaf*)

Jonquil narcissi (group 7). The jonquils are derived from *N. jonquilla*, and are 12–18 in (30–45 cm) tall, with dark green leaves, similar to those of rushes, and 2–6 scented flowers per stem, 1$^{1}/_{2}$–2$^{1}/_{2}$ in (4–6 cm) across, with a large perianth and low corona. Varieties include 'Suzy,' with bright yellow flowers and deep orange corona, and 'Trevithian,' with lemon-yellow flowers.

Tazetta narcissi (group 8). Derived from *N. tazetta*, these narcissi are 14–18 in (35–45 cm) tall and have 4–8 small, highly scented flowers per stem. The most popular varieties are 'Cragford,' with white flowers and scarlet corona; 'Geranium,' with white flowers and orange-red corona; and 'Paper White,' with white flowers.

Poeticus narcissi (group 9). Derived from *N. poeticus*, these narcissi are 14–18 in (35–45 cm) tall, and have normally single, highly scented, flowers with a white perianth and small, flat corona with a red margin. 'Actaea' has white flowers and bright yellow corona.

Botanical species, natural varieties and wild hybrids of narcissi (group 10). This group comprises all the wild species that originated the garden varieties. They are as a rule small plants with narrow or cylindrical leaves and one flower per stem. They include *N. bulbocodium*, *N. cyclamineus*, *N. poeticus*, *N. pseudonarcissus*, *N. tazetta* and *N. triandrus*. The principal cultivated species are described separately.

Miscellaneous (group 11). This group comprises all hybrids and varieties not otherwise classified, as for example 'Gold Collar' and 'Square Dance,' including split corona or orchid-flowered daffodils.

Flowering period The majority of narcissi and daffodils flower in spring. There are, however, some uncommon autumn-flowering species.

Cultivation Cultivated since A.D. 1500, narcissi are not particularly demanding plants. They grow well in sunny positions or in partial shade, in fertile soil rich in organic material and perhaps given some bonemeal. They do not develop properly in acid soil and are seriously harmed by standing water. Fresh manure should be avoided. Plant the bulbs from late summer to early autumn 3–6 in (8–15 cm) deep and 4–6 in (10–25 cm) apart, depending on how they are to be used and the dimensions of the plants. It is extremely important not to damage the leaves, which live for about a month after the last flowers fade. If the leaves are cut too soon the plant may die, or at best will not accumulate the necessary reserves to flower the following year.

The smaller species and varieties are suitable for the rock garden while the bigger ones are ideal for the border and create a better effect if planted in small groups or naturalized in grass.

Daffodils can also be grown indoors in pots or bowls. The Tazetta narcissi are particularly good for this purpose. Plant the bulbs September–October 4 in (10 cm) deep in a mixture of garden soil, peat and sand, or a potting compost or bulb fiber, and place in a cool, shady corner of the garden. After about 3 months put the containers in the cool greenhouse or bring indoors, where they should be kept for a few days in darkness, and then, when the shoots are 4 in (10 cm) high, get them gradually accustomed to light. They need a night-time temperature of 50°–56°F (10°–13°C).

Daffodils and narcissi may be attacked by numerous pests and diseases, including narcissus fly, bulb and stem eelworms, bulb rot, rust, and leaf spot.

Tazetta narcissus (group 8).

(*continued overleaf*)

Propagation   Like all the Amaryllidaceae, daffodils and narcissi are extremely sensitive to transplanting and should be disturbed as little as possible. Every 3–4 years, in July or August, the bulbs can be lifted from the ground, divided and replanted immediately.
Care   With the exception of the Tazetta narcissi, all plants are very hardy and tolerate winter frosts without problem.

Double narcissus (group 4): *Narcissus* 'Camellia.'

---

115   NARCISSUS CYCLAMINEUS

U.S. zone 5

Family   Amaryllidaceae.
Origin   Portugal, Spain.
Description   One of the loveliest narcissi, parent of many horti-cultural varieties. It is 6–8 in (15–20 cm) tall, with bright green leaves and single golden-yellow flowers $1^{1}/_{4}$–$1^{1}/_{2}$ in (3–4 cm) across, with a lanceolate, retroflex perianth, like the petals of the cyclamen, and a long, narrow trumpet.
Flowering period   March.

Cultivation   In nature the species is typically found in wet moun-tain meadows, and grows well in soil that is not too dry and in partly shaded positions. Plant the bulbs late summer–early autumn, 4 in (10 cm) deep.

Propagation   Every 4–5 years, after leaves have completely withered, lift the bulbs, divide and replant immediately.
Care   Like other species, *N. cyclamineus* can withstand winter frosts and does not like to be disturbed.

116 NARCISSUS POETICUS
Poet's narcissus

Family Amaryllidaceae.
Origin Southern Europe.
Description Poet's narcissus is 8–12 in (20–30 cm) tall and has an ovoid bulb, more or less glaucous leaves about $^3/_8$ in (8 mm) wide, and a single flower $1^1/_2$ in (4 cm) across, with a whitish membranous spathe and a perianth composed of pointed, oval, pure white segments, and a short corona, about $^3/_8$ in (9 mm) wide, yellow bordered with red. Among the numerous cultivated varieties is *recurvus*, with a retroflex perianth.
Flowering period April–May.
Cultivation In the Mediterranean region this narcissus grows wild in mountain pastures at 2,000–5,250 ft (600–1,600 m) altitude. It is the ideal species for naturalizing in fields, requiring a wet, compact, clay soil. Plant bulbs in autumn 8 in (20 cm) deep.
Propagation Every 4–5 years, after leaves have completely withered, lift the bulbs, divide and replant immediately.
Care This species withstands winter frosts without problem.

117 NARCISSUS PSEUDONARCISSUS
Lent lily

Family Amaryllidaceae.
Origin Western Europe from Scandinavia to Iberian peninsula.
Description This plant, 8–16 in (20–40 cm) tall, has an ovoid $^3/_4$–$1^1/_2$-in (2–4-cm) bulb with a brown tunic, erect scape, linear leaves as long as the scape, and a single flower with yellow perianth and trumpet of $^3/_4 \times 1^3/_4$ in (2×4.5 cm), with a toothed or rounded margin. There are also many cultivated varieties in colors ranging from white to orange-yellow.
Flowering period March–May.
Cultivation Plants are easy to cultivate and grow well in sun or light shade, in fertile soil that is rich in humus, fairly wet and not tending to dry out in summer. Plant the bulbs at the end of summer 2 in (5 cm) deep.
Propagation Every 4–5 years, after leaves have completely withered, lift bulbs, divide and replant immediately. They also reproduce from seed, flowering after 3–7 years.
Care The plants tolerate winter cold without problem and do not like to be disturbed.

118 NELUMBO NUCIFERA

(Syn. *N. speciosum*) **U.S. zone 7**
East Indian lotus

Family   Nyphaeaceae.
Origin   Tropical countries of Asia and Africa.
Description   This is an aquatic plant, with a whitish creeping rhizome from which sprout long, upright stalks that emerge from the water. The leaves are downy, 12–24 in (30–60 cm) in diameter, with their blades borne slightly above the water surface, and the stalk, sometimes over 3 ft (1 m) long, in the center. The flowers, on peduncles of 3–6 ft (1–2 m), are large, pinkish-white, with a receptacle in the form of a reversed cone.
Flowering period   June–August.
Cultivation   In warm climates this splendid plant can be grown in sunny pools or ponds 20–60 in (50–150 cm) deep, although it is not grown outdoors in Britain where you could, however, try growing it in a patio pond for the summer. They like stagnant water and a muddy bottom rich in organic materials. Plant the rhizomes horizontally in the bottom mud in spring. Alternatively, plant in pots that are then submerged.
Propagation   By dividing the rhizomes in spring.
Care   In the coldest climates the rhizomes can be left outdoors in winter if the water around them does not freeze or if the pool is drained completely and they are covered with an extremely heavy mulch. Otherwise, lift the rhizomes and store in a frost-free place indoors.
Other species   N. lutea.

---

119 NERINE BOWDENII

U.S. zone 6

Family   Amaryllidaceae.
Origin   Southern Africa.
Description   Plant 12–24 in (30–60 cm) tall, with tunicate bulb, linear leaves 12–16 in (30–40 cm) long, stiff scape terminating in umbel of 8–12 flowers consisting of strap-like segments of $2^3/_4$–$3^1/_4$ in (7–8 cm), slightly wavy and folded backward, pale pink with a darker central stripe. The species has originated many hybrids. 'Fenwick's Variety' is a large, strong form.
Flowering period   Late summer to late autumn.
Cultivation   The species is sensitive to winter frosts and survives outdoors only in temperate climates, in warm, sunny positions and in loose, fertile, well-drained soil. In cooler climates, it may need winter protection. It is also a good pot plant. Plant the bulbs $1^1/_4$–$1^1/_2$ in (3–4 cm) deep, early summer, in open ground or, if potted, in a mixture of equal parts peat, sand and soil, or a good loam-based compost. Water abundantly and feed every fortnight. The plant has a rest period in summer.
Propagation   In summer by separating the small bulbs which form alongside the bigger ones, or from seed in the greenhouse, with flowers after 4–5 years. The bulbs dislike being transplanted.
Care   Plants grown in containers should be sheltered in the cold greenhouse during the winter. Otherwise it is necessary to protect the ground with a generous mulch of straw and leaves.
Other species   N. crispa, N. flexuosa, N. sarniensis.

120 NOMOCHARIS SALUENENSIS

Family Liliaceae.
Origin Burma, Tibet, and China.
Description This species, similar to a lily, has an elongated bulb, without tunic, a stem of 24–36 in (60–90 cm), glossy lanceolate leaves, and 3–6 stellate, flattened flowers 3 in (8 cm) across, the petals white or pale pink, more darkly flushed at the tip, and with dark purple-red spots.
Flowering period Midsummer.
Cultivation This beautiful Himalayan plant grows well only in wet, cold climates, in partially shaded positions and in wet soil, rich with peat and some added sand. Plant the bulbs in spring 3–4 in (8–10 cm) deep and 12–16 in (30–40 cm) apart.
Propagation Transplanting may harm the plant; reproduction is therefore mainly from seed which is allowed to germinate January–February in the cold greenhouse.
Care The bulbs can withstand frost. They should be disturbed as little as possible.
Other species *N. aperta*, *N.* × *finlayorum*, *N. pardanthina*.

121 NUPHAR LUTEA
Yellow water-lily

Family Nymphaeaceae.
Origin Europe and Asia.
Description The yellow water-lily has a large rhizome set in the bottom mud, floating oval or spear-shaped leaves, generally with a wavy margin, a stalk one-quarter way up the blade, and flowers 1½–2 in (4–5 cm) across. These have 5 yellow sepals and numerous petals.
Flowering period June–August.
Cultivation Often found growing wild in stagnant or slow-flowing waters, the yellow water-lily can be grown in full sun in pools and ponds 8–12 in (20–40 cm) deep. Bury the rhizomes in spring in the fertile, clayey soil of the bottom.
Propagation By dividing the rhizomes in spring and immediately planting them out.
Care In cold climates the water should be drained in winter to avoid freezing and the bottom soil protected with leaves to keep it dry. (This is not necessary in Britain.)
Other species *N. advenum* is native to eastern North America.

122 NYMPHAEA ALBA
(European) white water-lily   U.S. zone 4

Family Nymphaeaceae.
Origin Europe and Asia.
Description This water-lily has a fleshy rhizome buried in the bottom mud, floating leaves, flat, whole and round, with a stalk one-third way up the blade, and flowers 4–5 in (10–12 cm) across, with 4 white sepals and numerous petals, in a spiral. There are many varieties suitable for cultivation.
Flowering period June–September.
Cultivation Plant rhizomes out in spring in the bottom of a pool, in water 6–40 in (15–100 cm) deep. The soil should be a clayey mixture spread over a 4-in (10-cm) layer of manure. Alternatively the water-lilies can be planted in a mixture of manure and clayey soil in wooden boxes or plastic planting baskets that are placed at the required depth in the pool.
Propagation Every 3–4 years, in spring, by dividing rhizomes, which should be kept for a month or so in water either indoors or in the greenhouse and then planted out.
Care In cold climates the water should be drained in winter to prevent freezing, and the bottom soil protected with leaves to keep it dry. (This is not necessary in Britain.)

---

123 NYMPHAEA RUBRA
Tropical red water-lily   U.S. zone 8

Family Nymphaeaceae.
Origin India.
Description This exotic water-lily has a fleshy rhizome, flat, heart-shaped, floating leaves with a toothed margin and a stalk about one-third way up the blade. The flowers are a dark purple-red and have upright petals. They are borne on peduncles that protrude from the water.
Flowering period Summer.
Cultivation Plant the rhizomes in spring in a sunny position at the bottom of a pool or pond, in water 6–40 in (15–100 cm) deep. Use a clayey soil covered with a 4-in (10-cm) layer of manure. Alternatively the water-lilies can be planted in a mixture of manure and clayey soil in wooden boxes or plastic planting baskets. In Britain this plant is not suitable for outdoor ponds, and should only be attempted in a heated pool in a greenhouse or conservatory.
Propagation Every 3–4 years, in spring, by dividing the rhizomes, which should be kept for a month or so in water or in the greenhouse and then planted out.
Care In cold climates the water should be drained in winter to avoid freezing and the bottom soil protected with leaves to keep it dry. If growing in a heated pool under glass, the plant can simply be left undisturbed.

124 ORNITHOGALUM THYRSOIDES
Chincherinchee   U.S. zone 7

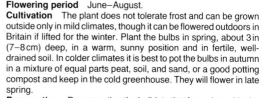

Family Liliaceae.
Origin Southern Africa.
Description In summer 1–3 flower scapes 20–24 in (50–60 cm) tall sprout from the round white bulb. The leaves are fleshy, green, 12 in (30 cm) long, and grow at the base of the plant. The dense racemes of flowers are white, stellate, with long orange stamens and a brown ovary.
Flowering period June–August.
Cultivation The plant does not tolerate frost and can be grown outside only in mild climates, though it can be flowered outdoors in Britain if lifted for the winter. Plant the bulbs in spring, about 3 in (7–8 cm) deep, in a warm, sunny position and in fertile, well-drained soil. In colder climates it is best to pot the bulbs in autumn in a mixture of equal parts peat, soil, and sand, or a good potting compost and keep in the cold greenhouse. They will flower in late spring.
Propagation By separating the bulblets that form alongside the bulbs, or from seed, with flowers after 4 years.
Care Bulbs planted outside need protecting in winter with a thick mulch of leaves and peat. (This is not, however, recommended for Britain.)

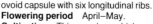

125 ORNITHOGALUM UMBELLATUM
Star of Bethlehem   U.S. zone 5

Family Liliaceae.
Origin Most of Europe, North Africa, Turkey, Syria, Lebanon, Israel, Cyprus.
Description This elegant member of the lily family has a pear-shaped, tunicate bulb, leaves $^1/_8$–$^1/_4$ in (2–6 mm) wide with a central white line, and corymbs of 6–20 flowers with lanceolate, star-shaped petals, white with a green stripe on the back. The fruit is an ovoid capsule with six longitudinal ribs.
Flowering period April–May.
Cultivation This species, which grows wild in fields up to a height of 4,000 ft (1,200 m), can be cultivated without any problem. It needs fertile soil with an addition of peat and leafmold. Plant the bulbs at the end of August about 3 in (7–8 cm) deep and in partial shade. The plant naturalizes freely and is ideal for the rock garden.
Propagation In late summer by separating the bulblets from the bulbs. The plant multiplies rapidly and can also be propagated from seed, with flowers after 3–4 years.
Care Once planted, the bulbs need no attention.

126 OXALIS ADENOPHYLLA

U.S. zone 8

Family Oxalidaceae.
Origin Chile.
Description This delicate-looking, low-growing plant has gray-green leaves composed of numerous leaflets, and scapes of 2–4 in (5–10 cm). When in bloom it forms a splendid cushion of funnel-shaped, five-petaled, lilac-pink flowers, 1¼ in (3 cm) in diameter.
Flowering period Early summer.
Cultivation Plant the rhizomes of this hardy species, ideal for the rock garden, in autumn or spring, 3 in (8 cm) deep and 4 in (10 cm) apart, in fertile, well-drained soil with added peat and sand, in a sunny position. It is advisable to give it a fertilizer high in phosphates when growth begins. The plant can also be potted in any good loam-based potting compost.
Propagation In late summer by dividing the rhizomes.
Care The plant survives outside all year round and needs no attention.

127 OXALIS CERNUA
(Syn. *Oxalis pes-caprae*)   U.S. zone 9
Bermuda buttercup

Family Oxalidaceae.
Origin Southern Africa.
Description This highly decorative bulbous plant, 8–12 in (20–30 cm) tall, forms carpets of glossy, palmate, slightly succulent leaves, and bright yellow campanulate flowers, about 1 in (2–3 cm) long, turned downward. 'Plena' has double flowers.
Flowering period Spring.
Cultivation Half-hardy species that can be cultivated outside only in zones with temperate winters. In cold climates grow in greenhouse. Plant the bulbs in March or September 3–4 in (8–10 cm) deep, in a sheltered, warm spot, in sun or partial shade, in well-drained soil, preferably with an addition of peat and leaf-mold. It can also be grown in pots of 10 in (25 cm) diameter.
Propagation After flowering by separating bulblets.
Care In mild climates, where the plant is grown outside, the ground should be covered in winter with a thick layer of leaves.

128 PANCRATIUM MARITIMUM

(Syn. *Hymenocallis maritimum*)   **U.S. zone 7**
Spider lily, Sea lily

Family   Amaryllidaceae.
Origin   Mediterranean coasts.
Description   This very beautiful shore lily has a large bulb, basal leaves $^3/_4$ in (1–1.5 cm) wide with a linear-lanceolate blade and a scape of 1$^1/_2$–2$^1/_2$ in (4–6 cm) which bears at the tip a membranous spathe and an umbel of 5–10 scented flowers with a perianth consisting of a greenish funnel-shaped tube and six white segments.
Flowering period   July–September.
Cultivation   The species grows wild on Mediterranean shores, doing well in sandy, thoroughly drained soil and in a warm, sunny position. In order for the bulb to mature fully a warm, dry period is essential after flowering. Plant the bulbs in autumn 6 in (15 cm) deep.
Propagation   In autumn by separating the bulblets that form alongside the bulb.
Care   During winter the bulbs can remain in the ground, but in cold climates, including Britain, a plentiful mulch of leaves, peat, or pulverized bark is necessary.

---

129 PARADISEA LILIASTRUM

(Syn. *Liliastrum album, Anthericum liliastrum*)   **U.S. zone 6**
St Bernard's lily

Family   Liliaceae.
Origin   Mountain regions of southwestern Europe.
Description   This plant, 1$^1/_2$–2$^1/_2$ in (4–6 cm) tall, has fleshy rhizomatous roots, an upright, smooth, cylindrical stem, 6–8 radical leaves, linear and grooved, 6–16 in (15–40 cm) long, and a terminal raceme of 5–10 single-sided flowers, similar to lilies, with white petals of 1$^1/_2$ in (4 cm) and yellow anthers.
Flowering period   June–July.
Cultivation   This splendid lily grows wild in sunny fields and meadows at heights of 2,600–6,000 ft (800–1,800 m). It can be cultivated successfully in a light, humus-rich soil in a partially shaded spot. Plant the rhizomes in autumn or spring 3 in (8 cm) deep. It is an ideal species for naturalizing in fields and is suitable, too, for the rock garden.
Propagation   By dividing the rhizomatous roots in autumn or spring, or from seed in the cold greenhouse, with flowers after 2–3 years.
Care   The plant is very tolerant of frost. In autumn cover the ground with a mixture of leaves and fresh manure.

130 PLEIONE FORMOSANA
(Syn. *P. bulbocodiodes*)   U.S. zone 8

Family Orchidaceae.
Origin Tibet, China, Taiwan.
Description This magnificent ground orchid has pseudobulbs 1 in (2.5 cm) tall, leaves with thick veins that appear after flowers, stems 6 in (15 cm) long, and flowers 3–4 in (8–10 cm) wide, with long, narrow petals, varying from white to mauve, and a funnel-shaped lip fringed at the margin, with brick-red or yellow spots. 'Alba' is particularly beautiful.
Flowering period January–March indoors and April–May outdoors.
Cultivation In zones with a mild climate it may be grown outside, in rock gardens, in sheltered positions. Plant in light, well-drained soil enriched with leafmold or peat, in a sheltered, partly shaded spot. Alternatively plant the pseudobulbs in pots in April–May, using a mixture of two parts potting compost and one part sphagnum moss. Apply liquid fertilizer every fortnight from June to September. Repot every 2–3 years.
Propagation At time of repotting by separating shoots that form at the base of the pseudobulbs or by collecting the pseudobulbs that drop after growth is completed.
Care Outside, in less sheltered positions, cover the plants with bell jars from October to April. Inside, keep in a shaded position during rest period.
Other species *P. humilis*, *P. praecox*.

---

131 POLIANTHES TUBEROSA
Tuberose   U.S. zone 8

Family Agaraceae.
Origin Mexico.
Description This plant has a tuber surrounded by smaller bulbs; an upright stem, 32 in (80 cm) tall, linear leaves of 18 in (45 cm) and spikes of white, waxy, highly scented flowers, with a perianth of $2^{1}/_{2}$ in (6 cm), at first tubular and then opening like a star. 'La Perla' (also sold as 'The Pearl') has double flowers.
Flowering period Late summer.
Cultivation It can be grown outside only in regions with a warm climate. Plant in late winter, in full sun, $^{3}/_{4}$ in (2 cm) deep, in fertile, well-drained soil with plenty of humus and in a very sheltered corner of the garden if you live in a warm climate. The inflorescences should be removed when they begin to fade. The plant can also be grown in a pot and brought outdoors for the summer. Watering should be very regular.
Propagation Seldom successful.
Care It is best to buy new tubers every year.

132 POLYGONATUM ODORATUM

(Syn. *P. officinale, Convallaria polygonatum*) **U.S. zone 4**
Solomon's seal

Family Liliaceae.
Origin Cold and temperate-cold zones of Europe and Asia.
Description The name of this species is derived from the presence on the white, knotty rhizome of characteristic seal-like depressions. The stem is upright, angular and two-winged, the leaves are elliptical, glaucous underneath, and the delicately scented flowers, single or in pairs at the leaf axils, are pendulous, with a perianth 3/4 in (2 cm) long, tubular, cylindrical, white with six greenish teeth.
Flowering period April–June.
Cultivation This Solomon's seal is widely found growing in broadleaved woods at altitudes of 650–5,000 ft (200–1,500 m). It can be grown easily in light, slightly acid soil with plenty of organic material, in a partially shaded spot. The roots, fairly superficial, may be damaged in periods of prolonged drought, in which case watering is necessary.
Propagation In spring by dividing the rhizomes.
Care The plant tolerates winter cold without problem, but it is helpful to apply a mulch of leaves in autumn.
Other species *P.* × *hybridum, P. biflorum, P. commutatum, P. japonicum.*

---

133 PUSCHKINIA SCILLOIDES

(Syn. *P. libanotica, P. sicula*) **U.S. zone 5**

Family Liliaceae.
Origin Caucasus, Asia Minor, Lebanon.
Description This small plant, not more than 8 in (20 cm) tall, has a rounded bulb, strap-like leaves and racemes of campanulate flowers, 3/4 in (1.5 cm) long, with a perianth of six light blue petals, each with a darker central stripe. 'Alba' has white flowers.
Flowering period Spring.
Cultivation This hardy species, which is suitable for rock gardens and also for small pots and bowls, likes sandy, humus-rich soil and fairly sunny positions. Plant the bulbs in autumn 3–4 in (8–10 cm) deep and 3–6 in (8–15 cm) apart.
Propagation In autumn by separating the bulblets that form around the adult bulbs and replanting at once, or from seed, again in autumn, in the cold greenhouse, with flowers after 4 years.
Care The plant tolerates frost.

Puschkinia scilloides 'Alba.'

134 RANUNCULUS ASIATICUS
Persian buttercup

Family Ranunculaceae.
Origin Asia Minor.
Description The characteristic tuberous roots of *R. asiaticus* are subdivided into a number of fleshy "claws." The stem is erect, 10–16in (24–40cm) tall; the light green leaves are deeply divided, disappearing in summer, and the abundant flowers, semi-double or double, 1¼–4in (3–10cm) across, vary from crimson to pink and yellow, according to variety.
Flowering period July.
Cultivation The vast *Ranunculus* genus comprises dozens of species but only this one, originating in the Middle East, has commanded much interest from growers. A very large number of hybrids has been derived from it. Plant the roots in the autumn, 2in (5cm) deep, with the "claws" facing downward, in fertile, well-drained soil and in a sunny position.
Propagation In autumn by dividing the roots or in spring from seed, with flowers after 2 years.
Care From U.S. zone 6 southward lift the roots from the ground in summer after foliage begins to yellow; dry off in the sun, then store in sand in a cool place until replanting in the autumn. In colder climates, plant in spring and store indoors over winter. In Britain *R. asiaticus* may survive a mild winter outdoors, but it is safer to lift and store in a frost-free place.

135 RECHSTEINERIA CARDINALIS

tender

Family Gesneriaceae.
Origin Brazil.
Description This lovely tuberous house plant, 10–18in (25–45cm) tall, has velvety, heart-shaped leaves, 4–6in (10–15cm) long, and numerous tubular, bright red flowers, 2in (5cm) long.
Flowering period Throughout summer.
Cultivation Plant the tubers March–April in shallow pots or bowls, in a mixture of two parts peat, one part potting soil and one part sand or any good proprietary compost. Keep them at a temperature of 65°–75°F (18°–24°C) in moist surroundings where they do not receive direct sunlight. Water regularly and frequently and feed throughout the spring and summer every fortnight. In autumn, when flowering is over, gradually suspend watering and feeding.
Propagation In February–March by dividing the tubers, or from seed.
Care During the winter leave the tubers in pots, completely dry, at a temperature of 54°–59°F (12°–15°C).
Other species *R. leucotricha.*

136 ROMULEA BULBOCODIUM
(Syn. *Crocus bulbocodium*)

Family Iridaceae.
Origin Mediterranean coasts from Gibraltar to Black Sea.
Description This plant has a pear-shaped corm with brown, papery tunics; a stem of 1¼–6 in (3–15 cm), semi-cylindrical; linear leaves that are longer than the stem; and a perianth consisting of a short tube, yellow and downy at the throat, and elliptical segments yellow at the base and then violet streaked with yellow, violet and green.
Flowering period March–May.
Cultivation The species grows wild in dry fields and woodlands of the Mediterranean basin and is ideal for rock gardens or small beds and borders. In cold climates it grows well only in positions that are very sunny during the flowering period. Plant the bulbs in groups, in autumn, 2 in (5 cm) deep, in the open ground or in pots, in sandy, well-drained soil.
Propagation In late summer by separating the bulblets, or from seed.
Care The bulbs can be left in the ground all year round, but in cold climates and positions not fully exposed to the sun it is advisable, in autumn, to protect the soil with straw and leaves.
Other species *R. clusiana*, *R. crocea*, *R. requienii*.

137 SCHIZOSTILIS COCCINEA
Kaffir lily

Family Iridaceae.
Origin Southeastern Africa.
Description This rhizomatous species, 30–36 in (75–90 cm) tall, has long, sword-shaped, pale green leaves and racemes of stellate flowers, 1½–2 in (4–5 cm) wide, crimson or pink, according to variety. 'Major' has dark red flowers that are larger than those of the typical species, and 'Viscountess Byng' has bright pink flowers that are stronger than those of the typical species.
Flowering period Autumn.
Cultivation Since it does not tolerate winter cold, this elegant plant grows well only in sunny positions adequately sheltered from cold winds. Plant the rhizomes in spring, 1 in (2.5 cm) deep and 10 in (25 cm) apart, in cool, fertile soil. Every year, in April–May, it is best to cover the ground with peat and leafmold to maintain high humidity. The late flowering habit creates a heavy demand for the cut flowers.
Propagation In spring, every 2–3 years, lift the rhizomes from the ground, divide them, making sure that each piece has at least 3–4 shoots, and replant them immediately.
Care During winter the rhizomes can remain outside but need the protection of a mulch of ferns and straw in cold areas, though this may not be necessary in mild parts of Britain.

138 SCILLA BIFOLIA

Family Liliaceae.
Origin Central and southern Europe, Turkey.
Description Bulb ½–¾ in (1–2 cm) wide; upright stem, generally one per bulb; 2–3 linear-lanceolate leaves sprouting from ground in later winter or early spring; and a raceme of 6–10 stellate flowers with violet-blue, sometimes pink or white, petals.
Flowering period March–April.

Cultivation This hardy species withstands winter cold. Plant the bulbs in autumn 2 in (5 cm) deep and 8–10 in (20–25 cm) apart, in cool, humus-rich, well-drained soil, in a warm, sunny position and leave undisturbed for several years. The plant is suitable for the rock garden.
Propagation In late summer by separating the bulblets, or from seed, with flowers after 2–3 years.
Care The bulbs survive in the ground all year round without problem.

139 SCILLA PERUVIANA
(Syn. *S. sicula, S. vivianii*)
Cuban lily

Family Liliaceae.
Origin Western Mediterranean.
Description This species has a large bulb of 1½–2¾ in (4–7 cm); a cylindrical, glabrous scape; lanceolate, fleshy leaves, with a tip; and dense umbels of flowers with glowing petals, violet with a purple-green line on the back. It is incorrectly called the Peruvian scilla.
Flowering period May–June.

Cultivation The plant, which grows wild in Mediterranean woodlands and on grassy slopes, is not too tolerant of cold and therefore can be cultivated outside only in temperate climates. Plant the bulbs at the end of summer 2 in (5 cm) deep and 8 in (20 cm) apart, in cool, humus-rich, well-drained soil, in a warm, sunny position. The bulbs can also be grown in pots, in which case use a mixture of equal parts soil, peat, and sand, or any good potting compost, and keep for 2 months in a cold, dark place, then put in a cool indoor position.

Propagation In late summer by separating the bulblets, or from seed, with flowers after 2–3 years.
Care The bulbs can stay in the ground throughout the year but in cold, wet climates the soil should be protected in winter with a plentiful mulch of straw and leaves. (This should not be necessary in Britain.)

140 SCILLA SIBIRICA
Siberian squill

U.S. zone 4

Family Liliaceae.
Origin Russia, Caucasus.
Description A popular bulbous plant with a slender stem, 8 in (20 cm) tall, linear leaves and loose racemes of pendulous, stellate, campanulate, deep blue flowers, 1 in (2.5 cm) long. 'Alba' has white flowers and 'Atrocoerulea' (better known as 'Spring Beauty') larger and sturdier blue flowers.
Flowering period April–May.
Cultivation A hardier species than the previous one, it tolerates winter cold without problem. Plant the bulbs in autumn 2 in (5 cm) deep and 8–10 in (20–25 cm) apart, in cool, humus-rich, well-drained soil, in a warm, sunny position. The plant is suitable for the rock garden.
Propagation At end of summer by separating the bulblets, or from seed, with flowers after 2–3 years.
Care The bulbs can remain in the ground all year round without problem.

Scilla sibirica 'Atrocoerulea.'

141 SCILLA TUBERGENIANA
(Syn. *S. mischtschenkoana*)

U.S. zone 5

Family Liliaceae.
Origin Northwestern Iran.
Description This small plant from the Middle East, 3–4 in (8–10 cm) tall, has a rounded bulb with a gray tunic, shorter and broader leaves than those of other scillas, and loose racemes of a few large-belled flowers, 1¹/₂ in (4 cm) across, pale blue with darker stripes. The flowers appear before the leaves.
Flowering period February–March.
Cultivation A very hardy species that withstands frost without problem. Plant the bulbs in autumn 2 in (5 cm) deep and 8–10 in (20–25 cm) apart, in cool, well-drained soil, with an addition of leafmold and peat, in a warm, sunny position. The plant dislikes periods of prolonged drought. It is suitable for the rock garden.
Propagation At end of summer by separating the bulblets, or from seed, with flowers after 2–3 years.
Care The bulbs can stay in the ground all year round.

142 SINNINGIA SPECIOSA

(Syn. *Gloxinia speciosa*)   **tender**
Gloxinia

Family Gesneriaceae.
Origin Brazil.
Description Relatively recently detached from the genus *Gloxinia*, but retaining the common name, this beautiful tuberous plant is 10–12 in (25–30 cm) tall, and has fleshy, velvety, dark green leaves and campanulate flowers, 3–6 in (8–15 cm) across, single or double, in colors ranging from white to red, pink and violet. As a rule, groups of large-flowered hybrids are grown. They include 'Emperor Frederick,' with white-edged scarlet flowers; 'Emperor William,' purple-blue with white-edged lobes; and 'Mont Blanc,' white.
Flowering period Summer.
Cultivation The gloxinia grows well only in warm, humid climates and is therefore best grown as a greenhouse or house plant in countries like Britain. Plant the tubers February–March in a mixture of sand, peat and soil, and keep at a temperature of 65°–75°F (18°–24°C) in a shaded position. Watering and feeding should be moderate at first and then frequent throughout the flowering period. When the leaves begin to wither, gradually slacken both operations and allow the plant to rest until the next growing season.
Propagation From seed, in March, with flowers after 6–7 months (the method most commonly used) or, at any season from leaf cuttings or division of tubers.
Care During winter the tubers are kept in pots, completely dry, at a temperature of 50°–65°F (10°–18°C).
Other species *S. eumorpha, S. regina.*

---

143 SMITHIANTHA CINNABARINA

(Syn. *Naegelia cinnabarina*)   **tender**
Temple bells

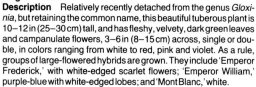

Family Gesneriaceae.
Origin Central and South America.
Description This plant has scaly, cylindrical rhizomes, stems 8–24 in (20–60 cm) tall, cordate leaves covered with dark red down, and terminal pendulous racemes of numerous tubular flowers, red with white speckles.
Flowering period Staggered flowering from early summer to late winter.
Cultivation This species is very demanding about temperature and humidity, and does well only in the greenhouse. In January–February plant the rhizomes in a mixture of potting soil, sand and peat, and keep the pots in a warm, dark place until the first shoots appear. Then move them into the light, but sheltered from direct sun; water abundantly and feed once a month with liquid fertilizer. In autumn–winter, when flowering is over, gradually suspend both operations.
Propagation When flowering is over by dividing the rhizomes, or in May–June from leaf cuttings or seed.
Care During the rest period keep the rhizomes dry in their pots.
Other species *S. multiflora, S. zebrina* and hybrids.

Smithiantha cinnabarina 'Orange King.'

144 SPARAXIS TRICOLOR
Wand flower, Harlequin flower   **U.S. zone 9**

Family Iridaceae.
Origin Southern Africa.
Description Plant 12–18 in (30–45 cm) tall, with a corm, lance-olate leaves and flowers 1½–2 in (4–5 cm) across. Known as "Harlequins" in southern Africa, where the species is indigenous, because the six broad, flat petals take on such a vast range of colors. There are many horticultural varieties that are usually grown as mixtures.
Flowering period Late spring–summer.
Cultivation Fairly sensitive to frost, this plant can be grown out-side only in mild climates. Plant the corms in autumn in fertile, well-drained soil, adequately protected from wind, and in full sun. Water plentifully and feed regularly during entire growing period. The flowers are suitable for cutting.
Propagation In autumn by separating the small corms that form alongside the larger ones.
Care When the leaves wither, in summer, lift the corms from the ground, dry off and keep them dry until it is time to replant them.

145 SPREKELIA FORMOSISSIMA
(Syn. *Amaryllis formosissima*)   **tender**
Jacobean lily

Family Amaryllidaceae.
Origin Mexico and Guatemala.
Description Plant 12–18 in (30–45 cm) tall, with a large oval bulb protected by a black tunic, linear leaves 12 in (30 cm) long, and one (rarely two) pink flower scape bearing a single funnel-shaped flower 4 in (10 cm) long, bright red with the three upper petals broader.
Flowering period Late spring–early summer.
Cultivation The species does not tolerate frost and is best grown in a pot or outside only in mild climates. Plant the bulbs end of summer in a pot in good soil, with the tips showing. If outdoors, plant in spring, when there is no further risk of frost, 4–6 in (10–15 cm) deep, in a sunny position. Water plentifully in growing period and feed fortnightly with liquid fertilizer.
Propagation In autumn by separating the bulblets, or in spring from seed in cold greenhouse.
Care During winter the bulbs should be left in their pots in a cool, dry place. If outside, lift them from the ground, dry off and keep in dry peat at 56°–61°F (13°–16°C).

146 STERNBERGEA LUTEA
Lily of the field

Family Amaryllidaceae.
Origin Mountains of Mediterranean region.
Description Plant 5–6 in (12–15 cm) tall, pear-shaped bulb with brown-black tunic, upright trigonal stem, grooved linear leaves, and single flower, yellow with perianth composed of a ¹/₄-in (6–8-mm) tube and spatulate segments.
Flowering period September–October.
Cultivation Originally from the dry fields and woodlands of the Mediterranean basin, this plant is fairly resistant to cold and is ideal for the small border or the rock garden. Plant the bulbs late summer 4–6 in (10–15 cm) deep and 3 in (8 cm) apart in thoroughly drained soil and a sunny position. It can also be grown in pots.
Propagation At the end of summer by dividing the bulbs, or from seed in spring. Do not disturb them for the first 3–4 years.
Care The bulbs may be left in the ground throughout the year, but in cold climates it is best to provide a winter mulch of straw or leaves. (This is not necessary in Britain.)
Other species *S. clusiana, S. fischeriana.*

---

147 TIGRIDIA PAVONIA
Tiger flower

Family Iridaceae.
Origin Central and southern Mexico.
Description This lovely plant has a small, scaly, yellow bulb, stems 18–20 in (45–50 cm) tall, lanceolate, folded leaves and 1–6 very short-lived flowers, with three markedly larger outer petals, 4–6 in (10–15 cm) wide, with characteristic purple spots in the center. 'Alba' has white flowers with carmine spots; 'Canariensis,' yellow flowers with red spots; and 'Rubra,' orange-red flowers, although the tiger flowers are usually bought as mixed hybrids.
Flowering period Mid to late summer.
Cultivation It is a half-hardy plant that survives outside only in temperate climates; it can be grown outdoors in the summer easily in Britain, but must be lifted for the winter. Plant the bulbs in April, 3–4 in (8–10 cm) deep, in fertile, well-drained soil and in full sun. It can also be pot-grown, in which case give an initial covering of soil and peat, and feed regularly with a liquid fertilizer.
Propagation In spring by separating the small bulbs that form alongside the bigger ones, or from seed in the greenhouse, with flowers after 1–2 years.
Care In colder areas, mulch well in the autumn. North of U.S. zone 6, lift the bulbs in the autumn, dry off and store indoors until spring. In Britain it is best to lift the bulbs.

148 TRILLIUM GRANDIFLORUM
Wake robin

Family Trilliaceae.
Origin Eastern regions of United States.
Description Plant 16–20 in (40–50 cm) tall, with a short rhizome and a single verticil of three ovate leaves, 4–6 in (10–15 cm) wide, light green at the tip of the stem. The flowers are white, flushed bright pink, single, three-petaled, 1½ in (4 cm) across. 'Plenum' has double flowers. There are also varieties with pink or white flowers.
Flowering period Spring.
Cultivation This fairly hardy species likes shade and needs cool, sandy, well-drained soil, perhaps with an addition of peat and leafmold. Feed annually in autumn with a surface layer of fresh manure. Plant the rhizomes in late summer 4 in (10 cm) deep and 6 in (15 cm) apart.
Propagation At the end of summer by dividing the rhizomes, which should be replanted at once, or in spring from seed in greenhouse, with flowers after 4–5 years.
Care In cold climates it is wise to cover the ground in winter with a generous mulch of straw or leaves. (This is not necessary in Britain.)

149 TRILLIUM SESSILE

Family Trilliaceae.
Origin United States.
Description Rhizomatous plant 6–12 in (15–30 cm) tall, with a single verticil of three dark green leaves streaked with gray at tip of stem, and sessile, deeply scented flowers, about 3 in (7–8 cm) across, with long, narrow reddish-brown petals.
Flowering period April–May.
Cultivation Some requirements and growing procedures as for *T. grandiflorum*. Plant the rhizomes late summer 4 in (10 cm) deep and 4 in (10 cm) apart, in cool, sandy, well-drained soil, perhaps with addition of peat and leafmold. Feed in autumn with a surface layer of fresh manure.
Propagation At the end of summer by dividing the rhizomes, which should be replanted at once, or in spring from seed in greenhouse, with flowers after 4–5 years.
Care In cold climates it is wise to cover the ground in winter with a generous mulch of straw or leaves. (This is not necessary in Britain.)

150 TRITELEIA HYACINTHINA
(Syn. *Brodiaea lactea*)   U.S. zone 6

Family Liliaceae.
Origin Western America.
Description This lovely cormous plant has a stem 14–16 in (35–40 cm) tall, filiform leaves and umbels 3–4 in (8–10 cm) across of 20–30 milk-white flowers, sometimes veined in pink.
Flowering period End of spring, summer.
Cultivation Fairly resistant to winter cold, provided adequately protected; it cannot tolerate standing water and therefore needs light, sandy, well-drained soil. Plant the corms in September–October 4–6 in (10–15 cm) deep and 2–4 in (5–10 cm) apart, in a warm, sunny, sheltered position. The plant can also be pot-grown in sandy soil, and left to rest after flowering.
Propagation In March from seed, left to germinate in the greenhouse, flowering after 3–5 years; or in autumn by separating the small corms that form alongside the bigger ones.
Care The corms can be left in the ground throughout the year but in colder zones it is advisable to protect them in winter with a plentiful mulch of straw or leaves.

151 TRITELEIA LAXA
(Syn. *Brodiaea laxa*)   U.S. zone 6

Family Liliaceae.
Origin North America.
Description The plant has a corm; stiff, bare stems 20–24 in (50–60 cm) tall; ribbon-like leaves; and terminal umbels 1½ in (4 cm) wide, of funnel-shaped flowers, purple-blue with characteristic blue anthers. 'Queen Fabiola' has dark violet flowers.
Flowering period Late spring, summer.
Cultivation This half-hardy plant grows well in perfectly drained soil. Plant the corms in September–October, in groups, 4–6 in (10–15 cm) deep and 2–4 in (5–10 cm) apart, in a warm, sunny position. The stiff stems make it ideal for cut flowers.
Propagation In March from seed, left to germinate in the greenhouse, flowering after 4–5 years; or in autumn by separating the cormels from the corms. The latter operation should be carried out every 2–3 years.
Care The corms can be left in the ground all year round, but in climates subject to winter frost it is best to protect with a plentiful mulch of straw or leaves. In Britain it should be sufficient to plant them in a warm, sheltered position in the garden.

152 TRITONIA CROCATA

Family Iridaceae.
Origin Southern Africa.
Description This cormous plant has a stem 20–24 in (50–60 cm) tall; narrow, sword-like leaves; and spikes of 5–6 funnel-shaped flowers, 1½ in (4 cm) across, varying in color depending on the variety. 'Isabella' has pink flowers flushed with yellow; 'White Glory,' white flowers; 'Princess Beatrix,' deep orange flowers.
Flowering period Summer.
Cultivation This species is usually grown in pots or, in warm climates, outside in light, well-drained soil. Plant the corms in open ground in a sunny position in spring, or pot in the cold greenhouse in September–October, 5 corms to a pot of 5½ in (14 cm) diameter. Water the pots regularly and maintain a temperature of 41°–50°F (5°–10°C), then bring outdoors when the weather improves.
Propagation In autumn by separating the small corms that form alongside the bigger ones.
Care Shelter the pots during the winter. Mulch corms planted outdoors, though it is not wise to leave the corms out for the winter in Britain.

---

153 TROPAEOLUM POLYPHYLLUM
Wreath nasturtium

Family Tropaeolaceae.
Origin Chile, Argentina.
Description This plant has a prostrate habit; creeping rhizomes and stems; downy, deeply lobate silver leaves; and funnel-shaped yellow flowers, sometimes flushed with orange, ½ in (1.5 cm) across, with a long spur.
Flowering period Early to mid summer.
Cultivation The plant survives in the open only in mild climates, needing a warm, sunny, sheltered position in light, well-drained soil. Plant the rhizomes in April just below the surface. The plant grows rapidly and should be fed every year in spring with manure or other organic fertilizer. It is suitable for dry walls.
Propagation In autumn by dividing the rhizomes, from seed or from cuttings.
Care In mild climates the plant can be left in the ground throughout the year, provided it is given a mulch of straw or leaves. Otherwise the rhizomes may be lifted and kept in a dry place from October to March.

154 TROPAEOLUM SPECIOSUM
Flame flower, Vermilion nasturtium   **U.S. zone 9**

Family Tropaeolaceae.
Origin Chile.
Description Climbing or prostrate plant, with creeping rhizomes, thin stem, lobate leaves and numerous bright scarlet flowers, 1¹/₂in (4cm) across. The plant grows to a height of about 15ft (4.5m).
Flowering period July–September.
Cultivation Not always easy to acclimate, this plant needs cool, acid or neutral, moist but well-drained soil, in a shady position. Plant the rhizomes in spring in open ground or, during the rooting phase, in pots under glass. The plant should be mulched every year with manure. It dislikes intense heat and is very susceptible to polluted air. Ideal for covering pergolas and trellises in shady, cool places.
Propagation In autumn by dividing the rhizomes, from seed or from cuttings.
Care During winter the plant can stay outdoors but the ground should be suitably protected with leaves or straw.

---

155 TULBAGHIA FRAGRANS
U.S. zone 9

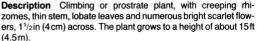

Family Liliaceae.
Origin Southern Africa.
Description Bulbous plant with upright stems 12in (30cm) tall; linear, persistent leaves 12in (30cm) long; and globose umbels of 20–30 small lavender-blue flowers, delicately scented.
Flowering period Throughout summer.

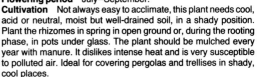

Cultivation The species is suitable for growing outdoors only in warm, sheltered places. It needs a light, sandy, thoroughly drained soil and a position in full sun. Plant the bulbs in spring or autumn just below ground and 8–12in (20–30cm) apart. The plant can also be grown indoors in pots.

Propagation In autumn by separating the small bulbs which form alongside the bigger ones. It is best to repeat the operation every 4–5 years.
Care During winter the plant can remain in the ground but should be given adequate protection. In Britain they are best lifted.

156 Genus TULIPA
Tulip

U.S. zone 3

Family Liliaceae.

Origin Europe, North Africa, temperate western and central Asia, especially mountain regions of Asia Minor, Iran, Caucasus and Turkestan. Hybrids of horticultural origin.

Description Tulips are perhaps the most popular of all spring-flowering garden plants, admired over the centuries for their bright colors and characteristic cup shape. They have a medium-sized bulb, rounded at the base and pointed at the top, with a brown tunic, an upright, cylindrical scape and glaucous-green linear-lanceolate leaves. The flowers are, as a rule, terminal, single, and made up of six petals.

The classification of tulips has always created problems for botanists and has been repeatedly modified. Recently there has been reclassification, based on the shape of the flower, the flowering period and the origin, into 15 groups. The last of these is made up of wild species. There are some 4,000 registered varieties. The groups are as follows:

Early single tulips (group 1). Comprises tulips 10–24 in (25–60 cm) tall, with single flowers, which sometimes flatten out in the sun and bloom early to mid spring. Varieties include 'Apricot Beauty,' salmon-pink flushed with red; 'Brilliant Star,' scarlet-orange with a dark basal spot; 'Diana,' pure white; and 'Prince Carnival,' yellow flushed with red.

Early double tulips (group 2). Comprises tulips 10–16 in (25–40 cm) tall, with double flowers, often 2½–4 in (6–10 cm) wide, blooming early to mid spring. Varieties include 'Carlton,' dark red, suitable for forcing in February; 'Monte Carlo,' sulfur-yellow; and 'Schoonoord' (syn. 'Purity'), brilliant white.

Triumph tulips (group 3). Tulips 20–24 in (50–60 cm) tall, with conical flowers on sturdy stems, as a rule fairly resistant to bad weather. They flower early to late spring, later than the early single and early double. They are sometimes grouped with Mendel tulips in catalogs under the heading of Mid-Season Tulips. Varieties include 'Attila,' violet; 'Cassini,' deep red and highly resistant to bad weather; and 'First Lady,' lovely dark violet.

Darwin hybrids (group 4). These are among the biggest and showiest tulips, flowering mid to end spring. Varieties include 'Apeldoorn,' scarlet-orange; 'Holland's Glory,' beautiful bright scarlet with splendid foliage; and 'Tender Beauty,' delicate pure white with pink edge.

Late single tulips (group 5). Also known as May-Flowering, and in some catalogs you will find some varieties listed under Darwin tulips (not to be confused with Darwin hybrids). Comprises tulips 18–30 in (45–75 cm) tall, generally with broad calyx and frequently pointed petals. They flower late spring to early summer. Varieties include 'Balalaika,' deep red with a yellow base; 'Gander,' deep pink; and 'Queen of the Night,' reddish-brown, almost black, the darkest of all tulips.

Lily-flowered tulips (group 6). They have characteristically pointed and outward-curving petals, flower late spring and are rather delicate. Varieties include 'Aladdin,' orange-red with yellow base inside, crimson with golden border outside, and 'Mariette,' deep pink.

Above: *Tulipa* 'Keizerskroon' (group 1).
Below: *Tulipa* 'Elektra' (group 2).

Fringed tulips (group 7). Comprises tulips 24–32 in (60–80 cm) tall, with fringe-edged petals. Varieties include 'Burgundy Lace,' with fairly long, wine-red flowers and a delicate crystalline fringe at the tips of the petals, and 'Maja,' pale mimosa-yellow outside and deep yellow with bronze base inside.

Viridiflora tulips (group 8). Generally 10–12 in (25–30 cm) tall, with partly greenish petals. Varieties include 'Artist,' green flushed with pink and apricot, and 'Golden Artist,' golden-yellow with green streaks and frilled petals.

Rembrandt tulips (group 9). Similar to late single tulips but the petals are streaked as a result of a virus. Varieties include 'Absalon,' brown and yellow, and 'May Blossom,' pink and purple-brown.

Parrot tulips (group 10). They are 18–24 in (45–60 cm) tall, and similar to late single tulips but their petals are twisted with a frilly or fringed edge. They flower in May. Varieties include 'Black Parrot,' purple-black; 'Fantasy,' pink outside and salmon with white center inside; and 'Orange Favourite,' orange with green streaks and yellow base.

Late double tulips (group 11). Usually listed in catalogs as Peony-Flowered. They are up to 24 in (60 cm) tall and have showy double flowers on sturdy stems. They flower mid to end spring and are rather delicate. Varieties include 'Mount Tacoma,' with enormous white flowers; 'Orange Triumph,' orange with brown tints and yellow fringes; and 'Uncle Tom,' dark red.

Kauffmanniana tulips (group 12). These are small tulips, 4–10 in (10–25 cm) tall, derived principally from *T. kauffmanniana*, with stellate flowers, similar to water-lilies, 2 1/2 in (6 cm) across, generally bicolored. They flower early spring. Varieties include 'Daylight,' yellow and scarlet with streaked leaves, and 'The First,' white with gold base and red edges.

Fosteriana tulips (group 13). Mainly derived from *T. fosteriana*, these are 12–18 in (30–45 cm) tall, with very large, brightly colored flowers. Varieties include 'Cantata,' deep vermilion-red and bright green leaves, and 'Red Emperor,' enormous bright red flowers with yellow-bordered black base.

Greigii tulips (group 14). Tulips 8–16 in (20–40 cm) tall, derived principally from *T. greigii*, with lovely foliage, generally wavy and streaked purple-brown, and large flowers that bloom mid to end spring. Varieties include 'Cape Cod,' apricot with yellow edge outside and yellow-bronze inside, and 'Plaisir,' creamy-white with red stripes.

Botanical species (group 15). Cultivated wild species and closely related varieties. Some of the most commonly grown botanical species are dealt with separately.

Flowering period Early to late spring, according to variety.

Cultivation Tulips are generally very easy to grow and fairly tolerant of adverse weather conditions. Like all bulbous plants, they need light, fertile, well-drained soil. Plant the bulbs in mid-autumn to early winter 5–6 in (12–15 cm) deep, in a sunny position. In the shade they produce plenty of leaves, flower the first year and then quickly degenerate. In spring they need heavy watering in especially dry periods. Faded flowers should be removed, but take care not to damage the leaves until they die down completely.

Tulips are normally grown in cold climates but with a little attention can also be raised in warm regions. In the latter case, the bulbs should be kept at 39°–45°F (4°–7°C) for about 8 weeks from autumn to November–December before planting. (This is not necessary in Britain.) Always plant 6–8 in (15–20 cm) deep. Tulips

Tulipa kaufmanniana (group 12).

are subject to molds and viruses. Almost all varieties are suitable for beds and borders, for pots and tubs in the garden or on the patio, and for cut flowers. The smaller ones, such as the Kauffmanniana and Greigii hybrids, can be used in the rock garden.

Propagation By separating the bulblets in autumn or from seed in February, with flowers after 4–6 years.

Care In most U.S. climates and in Britain the bulbs can remain in the ground over the winter without protection. In climates with very hot summers, lift the bulbs when the leaves shrivel, dry off and keep until autumn in a cool place.

Tulipa 'Mariette' (group 7).

---

157 TULIPA BIFLORA

U.S. zone 3

Family Liliaceae.
Origin Southern Russia.
Description This small tulip, not more than 4–6 in (10–15 cm) tall, has narrow, gray-green leaves and stellate flowers, ³/₄ in (2 cm) across, white with the central part yellow inside and flushed green and pink outside. Each bulb produces up to 5 flowers.
Flowering period February–March.

Propagation This very hardy species, suitable for small beds and borders, for pots and, above all, for rock gardens, needs light soil and sunny positions. Plant the bulbs in autumn 3 in (8 cm) deep and 3 in (8 cm) apart. If the ground is suitable, the species naturalizes freely.

Propagation In autumn by separating the bulblets that form alongside the main bulb, or from seed, with flowers after 4–5 years.
Care The bulbs can be left in the ground all through the year and do not require any winter protection.

158   TULIPA CLUSIANA
Lady tulip

Family   Liliaceae.
Origin   Iran, Iraq, Afghanistan.
Description   This is one of the oldest known species. It has underground bulbs, is 12–16 in (30–40 cm) tall, with upright, narrow, gray-green leaves, and flowers of 1½–2 in (4–5 cm), with pointed petals, white inside with a basal violet spot and red with a white border outside.
Flowering period   April.
Cultivation   This plant, which has been cultivated since 1600 and is widespread in the Mediterranean region where it was introduced about three centuries ago, prefers light, well-drained soils and a very warm summer climate. Plant the bulbs in autumn 6–8 in (15–20 cm) deep and in a sunny position.
Propagation   By separating the bulbs which enable the plants to spread rapidly. The species produces practically no seeds.
Care   The bulbs can be left in the ground throughout the year and require no winter protection.

---

159   TULIPA FOSTERIANA

U.S. zone 4

Family   Liliaceae.
Origin   Central Asia.
Description   Plant 16–18 in (40–45 cm) tall, variable in appearance, with gray-green lanceolate leaves and scarlet flowers, up to 10 in (25 cm) across, with petals truncate at the tip. It originated the varieties described in group 13.
Flowering period   April.
Cultivation   This magnificent tulip was raised by the Dutch firm Van Tubergen, by which time, in some opinions, it had already been partly modified by cultivation. Like the majority of tulips of Asiatic origin, it needs a warm, well-drained soil. Plant the bulbs in autumn in a sunny position 6 in (15 cm) deep and 4 in (10 cm) apart. It is used principally for borders.
Propagation   In autumn by separating the bulblets from the main bulb, or from seed, with flowers after 4–5 years.
Care   The bulbs may be left in the ground all year round and require no winter protection.

160 TULIPA PULCHELLA

Family Liliaceae.
Origin Asia Minor.
Description This is a dwarf tulip, not over 6 in (15 cm) tall. It has narrow leaves and flowers of 1¼ in (3 cm) which open in the form of a star, violet or purple with a bluish, white-edged center. 'Humilis' has violet-pink flowers with a yellow center, and 'Violacea' has purple-violet flowers with a yellow center. Each stem bears up to 3 flowers.
Flowering period End March–April.
Cultivation Particularly suitable for rock gardens, this dainty plant needs light, well-drained soil and a warm, sunny, sheltered position. Plant the bulbs in autumn 3 in (8 cm) deep and 3 in (8 cm) apart.
Propagation In autumn by separating the bulblets from the main bulb, or from seed, with flowers after 4–5 years.
Care The bulbs can be left outside all year round but in cold climates it is best to protect the ground with leaves or straw. (This is not necessary in Britain.)

161 TULIPA TARDA
(Syn. *T. dasystemon*)

Family Liliaceae.
Origin Eastern Turkestan.
Description This small tulip, 4–6 in (10–15 cm) tall, has basal rosettes of narrow leaves and stellate flowers 2 in (5 cm) across, white with a yellow center. Each stem bears up to 6 flowers.
Flowering period April–May.
Cultivation This is perhaps the most suitable tulip for rock gardens. It needs light, preferably alkaline, thoroughly drained soil and warm, sunny positions. Plant the bulbs in autumn, in groups of 5–10, 5–6 in (12–15 cm) deep and 3 in (8 cm) apart. It can also be grown in pots.
Propagation In autumn by separating offset bulbs.
Care The bulbs may be left outside all year round without problem.

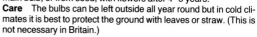

162 VALLOTTA SPECIOSA

(Syn. *Amaryllis purpurea, V. purpurea*) U.S. zone 9
Scarborough lily

Family Amaryllidaceae.
Origin South Africa.
Description This is perhaps the most beautiful of autumn-flowering bulbous plants. It is 24 in (60 cm) tall, and has an ovoid bulb, upright stem, linear, persistent leaves up to 18 in (45 cm) long, and 6–8 funnel-shaped scarlet flowers 3 in (8 cm) across, with a golden-yellow anther.

Flowering period Late summer–autumn.
Cultivation Suitable for growing in containers, in the cold greenhouse or indoors, it can survive outside only in warm climates, and is not recommended in Britain. Plant the bulbs up to the collar in spring, in a mixture of sand, leafmold, and peat. Water the containers plentifully during the growth period and feed every fortnight with a liquid fertilizer. In winter reduce the amount of water and suspend it completely from February to May when the plant rests.

Propagation In spring by separating the bulblets from the bulbs. Bear in mind that the plant, like all members of the family, reacts badly to transplanting.
Care Plants grown outside should be protected over winter with a generous mulch of straw and leaves. In Britain it is grown as a pot-plant indoors.

163 VELTHEIMIA CAPENSIS

tender

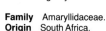

Family Liliaceae.
Origin Southern Africa.
Description A large bulb, partially above ground level, characterizes this species, which has tough leaves, wavy at the edges, arranged in a rosette at the base of the flower scape, violet speckled with yellow. Spikes of tubular, pendulous, yellow-pink flowers, 1 1/2 in (4 cm) long.

Flowering period End of winter.
Cultivation This species does not tolerate frost and should be cultivated in the greenhouse or indoors. Plant the bulbs in September, near the surface, in pots of 4–5 in (10–13 cm) diameter, in a mixture of equal parts sand, soil, peat and fresh manure – or use any good potting compost. Grow in a bright position. Water moderately and feed once a month with liquid fertilizer.

Propagation By separating the bulblets that form around the adult bulb, or from leaf cuttings.
Care After flowering, let the plant rest, keeping the bulbs dry until the following September.
Other species *V. deasii, V. glauca.*

164   WATSONIA BEATRICIS
Bugle lily   U.S. zone 8

Family   Iridaceae.
Origin   Southern Africa.
Description   This magnificent evergreen cormous plant, a close relation of the gladiolus, is 30 in (75 cm) tall and has an upright stem, sword-shaped leaves and dense spikes of bright orange flowers, 2 in (5 cm) across, with a long tube and well-opened corolla segments.
Flowering period   End of summer.
Cultivation   The plant does not tolerate cold and can be grown outside only in mild climates and in a warm, sunny position, if possible sheltered by a wall. Plant the corms outside in autumn, 4 in (10 cm) deep, in cool, fertile soil, or in the greenhouse. Feed with liquid fertilizer once a month and water regularly in summer, then reduce and suspend entirely during winter.
Propagation   In autumn by separating the cormels from the corm.
Care   During winter it is best to protect plants grown outside.

165   WATSONIA ROSEA
(Syn. *W. pyramidata*)   tender

Family   Iridaceae.
Origin   South Africa.
Description   This is perhaps the loveliest of the genus, 3–5 ft (1–1.5 m) tall, with a corm, sword-shaped leaves, ramified stems and broadly stellate, pink or mauve flowers, 1½–2½ in (4–6 cm) across.
Flowering period   June–July.
Cultivation   Found growing wild in South African mountain pastures periodically subject to fires, the plant does not tolerate cold and can be cultivated only in temperate regions. Plant the corms in spring 4 in (10 cm) deep in open ground, in fertile soil and a warm, sheltered position, or pot in the greenhouse in autumn. Feed once a month. The adult plants need staking.
Propagation   In autumn or spring by separating the small corms that form alongside the bigger ones.
Care   The corms should be lifted from the ground at the first frosts, dried off, cleaned and kept under shelter, in an airy spot, until spring.

166 ZANTEDESCHIA AETHIOPICA

(Syn. *Calla aethiopica, Richardia africana*) U.S. zone 9
Calla lily, Arum lily

Family Araceae.
Origin Tropical Africa.
Description This well-known and widespread species, 24–36 in (60–90 cm) tall, has large rhizomes, glossy basal leaves with a sagittate border, 8 in (20 cm) long and 4 in (10 cm) wide, and tiny yellow flowers, in a spadix inflorescence, covered by a showy funnel-shaped white spathe.
Flowering period End spring–early summer.
Cultivation The plant grows wild in tropical African swamps. Elsewhere it can be grown outside only in temperate zones, on fertile, moist or heavily watered soil during the summer, or on the banks of a pool or pond. In Britain, the variety 'Crowborough' is usually successful left outdoors in the milder countries. Plant the rhizomes in spring, 4 in (10 cm) deep or in water 4–12 in (10–30 cm) in depth, in a sunny position or in partial shade. The rhizomes can also be potted, in the greenhouse or indoors, in early autumn.
Propagation Late summer by dividing the rhizomes.
Care During winter the soil should be covered with straw or leaves to protect the roots from frost. Plants grown in pots should be sheltered.
Other species *Z. elliottiana, Z. pentlandii, Z. rehmannii.*

---

167 ZEPHYRANTHES CANDIDA

Zephyr lily U.S. zone 7

Family Amaryllidaceae.
Origin Argentina, Uruguay.
Description Plant 4–8 in (10–20 cm) tall, with a small tunicate bulb, linear, filiform, glabrous leaves, all at ground level, and a short, upright, hollow stem terminating in a single white flower, often flushed pink, 2–2$^1/_2$ in (5–6 cm) long, with orange stamens.
Flowering period End summer–early autumn.
Cultivation This is the hardiest species of the genus which, in temperate climates and if well protected in winter, can be grown outdoors. Plant the bulbs in autumn, 4 in (10 cm) deep, in light, well-drained soil, in sun or partial shade. It is suitable for the rock garden and can also be grown in pots.
Propagation In autumn by separating the small bulbs that form alongside the bigger ones.
Care In warm climates the plants can stay outdoors for the winter, but it is advisable to cover the soil with leaves or straw. In the north, dig bulbs in the autumn and store over winter.

GLOSSARY

Achene   Dry indehiscent fruit containing a single seed, in which the seed tegument does not adhere to the seed itself.

Agamic multiplication   Asexual reproduction accomplished by means of a plant part, such as bulb, stem or leaf. The new plant is identical to its parent.

Androecium   Male apparatus of the flower, consisting of the stamens.

Angiosperm   A flowering plant. The ovules are enclosed inside the ovary and the seeds inside a fruit.

Annual   Plant that completes its life within a single year.

Anther   Part of the stamen that contains the pollen.

Anticryptogamic   Substance used against fungi and bacteria.

Antiparasitic   Substance used against animal or plant parasites.

Apex   Terminal part of branch, leaf, root, etc.

Aphyllous   Stem or branch that does not carry leaves.

Axil   The point at which a branch diverges from the stem.

Bacterium   Single-celled organism without nucleus or chlorophyll.

Berry   Simple fleshy fruit with seeds buried in a fleshy or sugary mass.

Biennial   Plant that completes its life within two growing periods. During the first year the stem and leaves develop, during the second the flowers and fruit develop.

Bilabiate   Flower with calyx or corolla formed of two lips, an upper and a lower.

Bilobate   Plant organ divided into two lobes.

Bonemeal   Ground bone used as a fertilizer. A good source of phosphorus.

Border   A planting strip.

Bract   One of the small, scale-like leaves enclosing a flower bud before it opens. Sometimes bracts are large and highly colored, resembling petals, as in the poinsettia.

Bud   Small mass of plant tissue from which new organs or entire plants form.

Bulb   Underground organ composed of a very short transformed stem into which are fixed metamorphosed leaves that have protective and storage functions.

Bulbil   Small bulb produced above ground by a bulbous plant. The same term is used for plants with corms.

Bulblet   A small bulb produced below ground.

Caducous   Said of organs, typically the leaves, that fall off at an early stage; deciduous.

Calcareous   Soil containing high quantities of calcium.

Calyx   Outer covering of a flower, formed of one or more sepals.

Campanulate   Flower with bell-shaped corolla.

Capitulum   Inflorescence typical of the Compositae, consisting of numerous sessile flowers attached, one on either side, to a flattened receptacle and enfolded by bracts simulating a calyx.

Capsule   Dry dehiscent fruit, of which, when mature, opens to release seeds.
Carpel   Female unit in a flower containing ovary, style, and stigma.
Cauline   Pertaining to stem, as a leaf growing along the stem.
Cell   Fundamental structural unit of living organisms, composed of cytoplasm, one or more nuclei, and enfolded by a membrane. It is usually furnished with cell walls.
Cell wall   Stiff outer layer typical of plant cells and those of other microorganisms.
Cellulose   Carbohydrate of complex structure, the principal component of the cell wall of the majority of plants.
Channeled   Of a leaf, shaped like a channel or groove.
Chlorophyll   Green pigment of plant cells necessary for photosynthesis.
Chlorosis   Yellowing of leaves due to destruction or reduced production of chlorophyll.
Cirrus   Transformed leaf or branch, filiform in appearance, which can wrap itself around supports, enabling stemless plants to climb.
Clay   A very dense, heavy soil made up of particles with diameter of under 0.002 mm.
Clayey   Soil formed of a large percentage of clay. It is compact, difficult to work, and retains water, but has the advantage of holding nutrients well.
Cold greenhouse   Unheated greenhouse.
Collar   Part of plant between root and stem, with intermediate anatomical characteristics.
Compact   Used to describe a soil that is difficult to work, hardly permeable to air and water, usually composed of very fine, closely linked particles.
Compost (garden)   Mixture of decaying substances, such as dung, dead leaves, etc. It is used to fertilize soil.
Compost (for potting, etc)   A medium for sowing seeds or cuttings, or growing seedlings or pot plants. Although some are loam-based, most are nowadays peat-based.
Compound leaf   Leaf with blade divided into leaflets.
Coriaceous   Of stiff, tough consistency. Leathery.
Corm   An underground organ, composed mainly of stem tissue, specialized in performing a storage function.
Cormel   A small corm produced as an offset of the parent corm.
Corolla   The petals collectively; generally the most conspicuous part of the flower.
Corona   Rounded appendage of the corolla of certain flowers; typical of daffodils.
Corymb   A flat-topped flower cluster.
Cotyledon   Embryonic leaf, one or two in number, inside the seed, performing a storage function.
Cultivar   Named variety of a plant species raised in cultivation.
Cutting   A piece of a stem, leaf, etc., that is used in agamic reproduction.
Deciduous   A plant that loses its leaves at the beginning of the cold season.
Dehiscence   Opening mechanism of an anther, fruit or other structure, releasing the reproductive bodies contained in them, such as seeds, pollen, etc.
Dentate   With a margin consisting of pointed teeth.
Digging over   Deep digging of the ground with a spade or fork, with a view to turning over the clods.
Dioecious   Plant in which the male and female elements are borne by different individuals of the same species.
Disk   Collective formation of the tubular flowers of the capitulum in the Compositae.
Dissemination   Process of dispersing seeds or the fruits that contain seeds.

Dormancy   Period of rest for plants.
Drainage   Natural or artificial method of removing excess water from soil.
Drupe   Fleshy fruit with a single seed (e.g. a peach).
Dwarf   Of a plant, one of small dimensions and often creeping habit.
Embryo   Rudimentary new plant contained in the seed.
Ensiform   Sword-shaped.
Ephemeral   Plant or flower of very short duration.
Epigeum   Organ situated above ground.
Epiphyte   Plant that lives on another plant, for example a so-called air-plant such as an orchid. An epiphyte is not a parasite.
Evergreen   Plant that does not lose all its leaves at the beginning of the cold season and that retains its green foliage throughout the year.
Family   Systematic category between order and genus. The family name is derived from the name of one of the principal genera contained in it, and has the ending, in plants, -aceae.
Feed   Product of organic or mineral origin added to the soil to raise fertility.
Female flower   Flower provided only with a pistil.
Fertilization   Process of fusing the nuclei of the male and female gametes, thus forming a new individual.
Filament   The slender part of a stamen which supports the anther.
Flower   Reproductive organ of angiosperms. A complete flower consists of the perianth, formed of calyx and corolla, the androecium (the stamens) and the gynoecium (the pistils). In some cases the perianth may be absent or be formed of a single series of elements; in the latter case it is termed the perigonium.
Fruit   In angiosperms, the mature ovary, enlarged and transformed, containing the seeds.
Fungicide   Substance used against fungi.
Fungus   Plant organism without chlorophyll which can exist as a parasite or saprophyte.
Gamete   Reproductive cell which, following union with another gamete, originates a new individual. The process constitutes the basis of sexual reproduction.
Gamopetalous   Of a corolla, with petals wholly or partially joined.
Gamosepalous   Of a calyx, with sepals wholly or partially joined.
Genus   Systematic category between family and species.
Germination   Starting process of mechanisms associated with the growth of seeds, in buds and other structures.
Glabrous   Without hairs.
Growth period   Period of year in which a plant grows and reproduces.
Gynoecium   Female apparatus of flower, formed of many carpels.
Half-hardy   A plant which can live in the open for the summer but which, in cold climates, needs protection from frosts.
Haploid   Chromosomic arangement in which each type of chromosome is represented only once.
Hardy   A plant capable of tolerating winter cold without protection.
Herbaceous   Not woody.
Hermaphrodite   Flower provided with male and female reproductive organs on the same individual.
Honeydew   Sugary, sticky liquid secreted by aphids.
Horticultural (origin)   Variety created artificially by flower growers.
Hothouse   Greenhouse regularly heated, and kept very warm, suitable for raising particularly delicate plants.
Humus   Partially decomposed organic substance such as leafmold.
Hybrid   Individual originating from the crossing of different species or varieties.
Hybridization   Crossing of two different species or varieties.
Hypogeal   Organ or part of plant developing in ground.
Inforescence   Collection of flowers on a single axis.

Insecticide   Product of natural or artificial origin used against insects.
Intergeneric   Hybrid obtained by crossing plants belonging to two different genera.
Internode   Part of stem between two successive nodes.
Leaching   Removal by rainwater of mineral substances present in soil.
Leaf blade   Broad and flat part of the leaf.
Leaflet   Part of a compound leaf.
Limestone   Sedimentary rock constituted mainly of calcium carbonate.
Lymph   Watery solution containing minerals, sugars and other substances that circulate in a plant. The sap.
Male flower   Flower provided only with stamens.
Manure   Organic fertilizer originating from fermentation of animal droppings and organic material.
Metabolism   Sum of all the chemical processes that occur in a cell or living organism.
Monoecious   Plant that bears stamens and pistils on different flowers of the same individual.
Mulch   To cover the soil with various materials such as straw, peat, manure, etc. Also, a material such as those used to reduce loss of moisture from the soil, to restrict the growth of weeds, and to protect the soil from freezing.
Nematicide   Substance used to combat nematodes.
Node   Points on the stem in which one or more leaves arise.
Opposite   Of leaves, inserted in pairs in a node.
Order   Systematic category between class and family.
Organ   Structure composed of differentiated tissues. The stem, leaves and flowers, etc., of a plant are organs.
Organic   Relating to living organisms or to substances derived from living organisms.
Ovary   Lower part of pistil, inside which are the ovules. It is transformed into the fruit.
Ovule   Structure contained in the ovary, inside which is the female gamete.
Panicle   A branched inflorescence (strictly a branched raceme).
Papilonaceous   Of a corolla, consisting of one large outer petal, two side petals, and two interjoined inner petals.
Parasite   Organism that lives at the expense of another organism.
Peat   Often called peatmoss. A material originating from the accumulation of an undecomposed or partially decomposed organic substance in wet and cold places called peat bogs.
Peduncle   Stalk of a flower or inflorescence.
Pedunculate   Flower or fruit provided with a peduncle.
Perianth   External envelope of a flower.
Pericarp   The ripened wall of the ovary.
Pesticide   Substance used against plant or animal fats.
Petal   Part of flower, generally brightly colored, constituting the corolla.
Phyllo-   Prefix signifying leaf.
Pistil   Female structure, typical of angiosperms, comprising the ovary, the style and the stigma.
Planting out   Setting a plant out in its final growing position.
Plantlet   Young plant that develops after germination of seed.
Pollen   Grains produced by the pollen sacs of the anthers which originate the male gametes.
Pollen sac   Cavity of the anther containing the pollen grains.
Pollination   Process whereby the pollen passes from the anthers to the stigma.
Pricking out   Transplanting of the young plants born from seeds.
Propagation   The process of reproducing new plants from existing plants.
Prostrate   Of creeping habit.
Pubescent   Covered with tiny, soft hairs.
Pyrethrins   Active ingredient of insecticides based on pyrethrum, a

naturally occurring insecticide found in a species of chrysanthemum.

Raceme Inflorescence consisting on an elongated main axis into which are inserted the flowers, borne of pedicels of equal length.

Rachis Principal axis of a spike and of compound leaves.

Ray One of the flat, marginal petals of a flower.

Receptacle Portion of the flower axis into which are inserted the flower organs.

Rhizome Underground stem transformed and developing horizontally.

Rodenticide Product effective against rodents.

Root Part of the plant buried in the ground which serves to anchor it in the soil and to absorb and conduct water and mineral salts.

Rosette An arrangement of leaves or petals in a rose-like pattern.

Rotate Of a corolla, with symmetrical rays, like a wheel.

Sagittate In the shape of an arrowhead.

Samara Dry indehiscent fruit containing one or two seeds and furnished with a wing expansion which assists wind dispersion.

Sand Fraction of soil composed of particles with a diameter of 0.02-2 mm.

Saprophyte A plant that derives its nutrients wholly or partly from dead organic matter.

Scape Stem of herbaceous plant with a flower or inflorescence at the tip.

Seed Organ formed from the ripening of the ovule after fertilization and consisting of an embryo, storage substances and an outer coat.

Sepal Transformed leaf linked to the calyx.

Sessile A leaf without a stalk, or a flower or fruit without a peduncle.

Sheath Basal portion of leaf that enfolds a stem.

Shoot Aerial part of a plant.

Simple leaf Undivided leaf.

Soil Surface layer or earth's crust derived from the disintegration of rock due to climate and modified by the action of living organisms.

Spadix Inflorescence characteristic of Araceae, enfolded by a large bract called the spathe.

Spathe Transformed leaf, often colored, enfolding the inflorescence of Araceae.

Species Systematic category grouping individuals similar to one another. Species are designated by two names in italics, the first being the genus, the second the species to identify it within the genus.

Sphagnum Special kind of moss that grows in wet, cold places, such as peat-bogs, used as a potting constituent for a few plants.

Spike Inflorescence consisting of an elongated main axis into which are inserted sessile flowers.

Spur Posterior appendage of a corolla, cylindrical, straight or curved, of variable size.

Stalk Peduncle supporting a leaf.

Stamen Flower organ that produces pollen, generally made up of a filament and an anther. The stamens collectively constitute the androecium.

Stem Aerial part of a vascular plant, with functions of support, conduction, storage and sometimes photosynthesis. Underground parts with a similar anatomical structure (rhizomes, tubers, etc.) are also regarded as stems.

Stigma Expanded part of pistil on which pollen is deposited.

Stipule Foliar expansion found, in some species, at base of leaves.

Stolon Thin stem, creeping along ground, which may form roots arising from more than one point.

Stoma Tiny opening, generally present on the lower surface of leaves, through which gaseous exchanges are effected.

Style Filamentous body that links the ovary to the stigma.

Substratum Cultivated soil in which plants bury their roots.

Subspecies Subdivision of species.

Support A stake or similar object for propping up a plant.

Systematic category Unit of plant classification, such as family, genus or species.

Tegument   Protective layer enfolding the ovule from which the seed tegument originates.

Tepal   When flowers have inner and outer segments that appear the same and cannot be separately identified as petals or sepals. These are called tepals.

Tomentose   Covered by hairs.

Transplanting   Operation of transferring a plant from one place to another.

Tube   Underground stem enlarged and modified to carry out storage functions.

Tuberous root   Root transformed into a storage organ and no longer able to perform an absorbent function.

Tubular   Referring to a corolla, in the form of a tube.

Tuft   Group of stems with a common root apparatus.

Tunicate   Of a bulb, provided with a soft outer cataphyll and of membranous consistency.

Umbel   Inflorescence with single peduncles all inserted at the same point of the scape.

Unicellular   Organism composed of a single cell.

Unisexual   Flower without stamens or carpels.

Variegated   Of two or more colors.

Variety   Subdivision of a species which groups individuals distinguished by particular characteristics. Varieties may be natural or artificial. Varieties raised in cultivation are called cultivars to distinguish them from varieties that have arisen in the wild.

Veining   Network of conducting and supporting tissues in a leaf.

Vermiculite   Granular substance used as an ingredient in some potting and seed composts for rooting cuttings or germinating seeds.

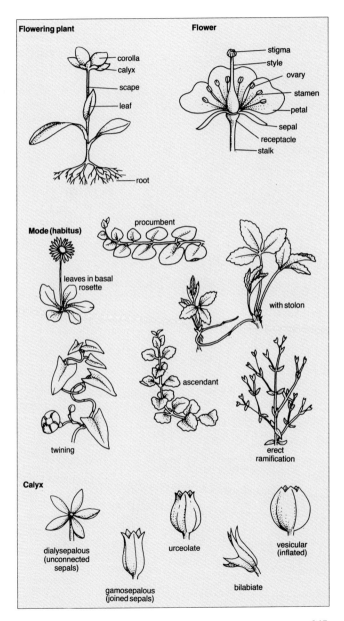

Flowering plant

- corolla
- calyx
- scape
- leaf
- root

Flower

- stigma
- style
- ovary
- stamen
- petal
- sepal
- receptacle
- stalk

Mode (habitus)

leaves in basal rosette

procumbent

with stolon

twining

ascendant

erect ramification

Calyx

dialysepalous (unconnected sepals)

gamosepalous (joined sepals)

urceolate

bilabiate

vesicular (inflated)

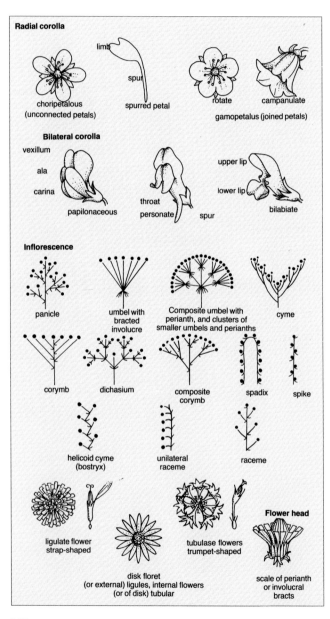

Radial corolla

choripetalous
(unconnected petals)

limb

spur

spurred petal

rotate

campanulate

gamopetalus (joined petals)

Bilateral corolla

vexillum

ala

carina

papilonaceous

throat
personate

spur

upper lip

lower lip

bilabiate

Inflorescence

panicle

umbel with
bracted
involucre

Composite umbel with
perianth, and clusters of
smaller umbels and perianths

cyme

corymb

dichasium

composite
corymb

spadix

spike

helicoid cyme
(bostryx)

unilateral
raceme

raceme

ligulate flower
strap-shaped

disk floret
(or external) ligules, internal flowers
(or of disk) tubular

tubulase flowers
trumpet-shaped

Flower head

scale of perianth
or involucral
bracts

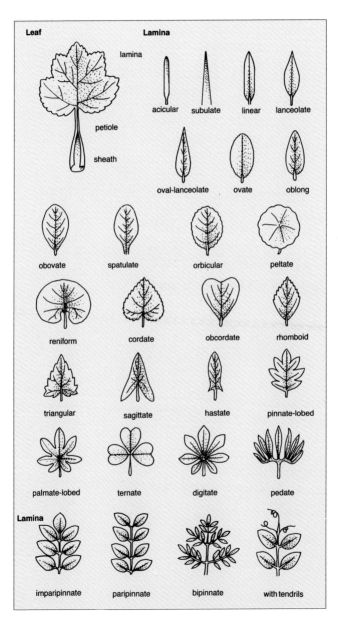

Leaf

Lamina

lamina

petiole

sheath

acicular | subulate | linear | lanceolate

oval-lanceolate | ovate | oblong

obovate | spatulate | orbicular | peltate

reniform | cordate | obcordate | rhomboid

triangular | sagittate | hastate | pinnate-lobed

palmate-lobed | ternate | digitate | pedate

Lamina

imparipinnate | paripinnate | bipinnate | with tendrils

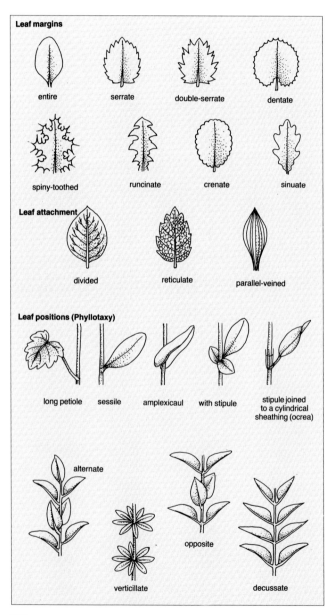

Leaf margins

entire   serrate   double-serrate   dentate

spiny-toothed   runcinate   crenate   sinuate

Leaf attachment

divided   reticulate   parallel-veined

Leaf positions (Phyllotaxy)

long petiole   sessile   amplexicaul   with stipule   stipule joined to a cylindrical sheathing (ocrea)

alternate

verticillate   opposite   decussate

BIBLIOGRAPHY

Crockett, J.U. *Bulbs*, Time–Life International, 1977.

Dykes, W.R. *The Genus Iris*, New York, Dover Publications, 1974.

Grey-Wilson, C.; Mathew, B. *Bulbs*, Collins, 1981.

Jekyll, G. *Lilies for English Gardens*, Antique Collectors' Club, 1982.

Mathew, B. *Dwarf Bulbs*, B.T. Batsford Ltd, 1973.

Mathew, B. *Larger Bulbs*, B.T. Batsford Ltd, 1976.

Mathew, B. *The Year Round Bulb Garden*, B.T. Batsford Ltd, 1978.

Papworth, D. *Illustrated Guide to Bulbs*, Salamander, 1983.

Porro, E. *I gladioli*, Milan, De Vecchi Editore, 1975.

Rix, M. *Growing Bulbs*, Croom Helm, 1983.

Rix, M. and Philips, R. *The Bulb Book*, Pan Books, 1981.

Royal Horticultural Society, *Dictionary of Gardening* (4 vols), Oxford University Press, 1965.

Schauenburg, P. *The Bulb Book*, Frederick Warne, 1965.

Springer, G. *How to Grow a Miracle*, Netherlands, John Boswell Associates Books, 1968.

Synge, Patrick M. *Collins Guide to Bulbs*, Collins, 1971.

Various authors, *Encyclopedia of Garden Plants and Flowers*, Reader's Digest Association, 1978.

Wright, M. *Complete Book of Gardening*, Michael Joseph, 1978.

INDEX

PICTURE SOURCES

All the photographs in this book have been supplied by the OVERSEAS Agency, Milan. The following are the original sources.

Introduction

Mondadori Archives, Milan: 17. – Internationaal Bloembollencentrum, Holland: 27. – Jacana, Paris: 20, 33, 34, 37, 238. – Moreschi, Sanremo: 2. – Overseas, Milan: 46–47. – Oxford Scientific Films, England: 8–9, 19, 23.

Entries

Mondadori Archives, Milan: 1. – A–Z Collection: 10, 12, 23, 39, 43, 44, 49, 52, 60, 62, 95, 97, 98, 99, 101. – A. Carrara Pantano, Verona: 45, 56, 81b, 94, 121, 138. – L. Cretti, Milan: 25, 27, 59a-b-e, 81a, 93, 96a-e, 104a-b, 114a-b-d, 125, 133, 134, 156a-b-c, 162. – Fabbri, Milan: 47. – R. Ferranti: 84. – S. Frattini, Milan: 17, 102. – Internationaal Bloembollencentrum, Holland: 24, 36, 64, 77, 80, 111, 141. – Jacana, Paris: 2, 3, 6, 7, 9, 15, 16, 19, 22, 28, 29, 30, 31, 34, 35, 37, 42, 50, 58, 59c, 61, 63, 65, 66b, 68, 70, 71, 72, 73, 74, 79, 82, 88, 89, 92b-c, 96d, 105, 106, 107, 112, 114c, 117, 118, 124, 128, 129, 131, 136, 137, 139, 144, 145, 146, 147, 149, 151, 156d, 159, 161. – Lamaison Nature: 5, 32b, 110, 122, 152. – J.L. Lemoigne: 96c. – Mazza, Montecarlo: 83. – Moreschi, Sanremo: 41, 85, 86, 123, 127, 143, 155, 167. – NHPA, England: 14, 40, 46, 48, 53, 54, 57, 59d, 66a, 69, 76, 92a, 96b-f, 104c, 108, 116, 140, 148, 156e, 166. – Oxford Scientific Films, England: 8, 11, 18, 21, 26, 33, 38, 75, 78, 87, 90, 103, 109, 115, 119, 126, 135, 142. – H. Smith, Horticultural Photographic Collection, England: 4, 13, 20, 32a, 51, 55, 91, 100, 113, 120, 130, 132, 150, 153, 154, 157, 158, 160, 163, 164, 165.